NOT SPECIAL

Special Stories from a Non-Special Forces Military

BRIAN SHOTWELL

NOT SPECIAL

To: Jen. You supported me through living and writing about all these stories. Forever.

TABLE OF CONTENTS

INTRODUCTION THIS IS FOR US

This is for the regular, everyday Joe. For those that tell strangers at a bar that they would have gone Special Forces buuuut [insert one of the following excuses: I'm color blind, regular unit wouldn't let them, too deadly, or paperwork was too much]. It's for that one cousin that always says they were gonna join the Army buuuut [insert similar excuse from above]. Heck, it's even for the ones that flat-out lie and tell the waitress at Applebee's or the bartender at Chili's that they're a Marine.

It's for the troops that are eating DFAC omelets and standing in pointless formations that could have been a text. I see you; I've been there. I'm laughing with you and at you all at the same time. It's for the 99.69% of people that signed the dotted line and still didn't turn into the Lone Survivor. This is for the everyday Joe, the bored-in-the-barracks PFC, the Sham Squad, and the NCO or officer that didn't take themselves too seriously. For those of us who made lifelong memories and for those that didn't make it out. For those that know what the mix of Axe body spray, feet, and cigarettes smells like. It's for anyone who has ever wanted to know what the military was actually like.

You could throw a rock and find an amazing story of valor, sacrifice, honor, and killing bad guys (and probably a movie to go with it). And we love all of those stories of courage and badassery. They're needed and for a lot of us, me included, we signed on the dotted line in hopes of becoming these people. Saving our buddies in battle and blasting as many bad guys as possible in the face along the way. We wanted to be Captain America.

But those stories are the top 1% of the 1%. They're told by the tip of the spear guys: Navy Seals, Green Beret's, Delta Force operators. You know, Mark Wahlberg in *Lone Survivor*. There's a million other people that are in the military that are living their day-to-day lives just trying to make it through their job like anyone else sitting in a cubicle at a nine-to-five. Those stories get lost in translation but are just as worthy as any other. Those people keep the big cog that is the military going on a day-to-day basis. They provide intel, cook food, do payroll, defend other soldiers in court, and the list goes on.

I got the chance to experience the "big Army," the one that didn't include a special forces tab on my uniform. I basically drafted myself. I was a fit, educated, single young man with a calling to something larger than myself. I saw enlisting as a duty to my country and to myself. So, I sold everything I owned and enlisted as a Military Police Officer. I wound up in a unit in Germany that was a stand-alone platoon that nobody in the outside world gave a shit about. That's alright though because I got to live and work with the funniest group of humans that I've ever been around. The people and stories that came from my time in the Army can't be forgotten. They're just too damn funny to not be told. The world deserves to hear about them. In fact, I actually lost half of this book and had to restart from a blank screen. Six months of hard work rewound back to day one again. There's going to be debauchery, characters that you wish weren't real, laughing so hard it hurts, and just plain idiocy along the way. So grab an 84 oz green Monster or Rip It and strap in. The big green weenie is coming.

PS: I definitely didn't send a single part of this book to the Department of Defense or wherever else you're "supposed to" for approval, so if you see my name on the news, you probably know why. Also, call my wife to make sure she knows I was arrested.

SECTION 1

MEPS AND BASIC TRAINING

CHAPTER 1: FAA (FEET, ASS, AXE)

"We'll sign you up to be a SEAL, bro."

–A recruiter in the middle of Alabama right now

Basic Training is everything you'd hoped it would be if you've ever seen any military movie like *Full Metal Jacket*. It is a shit show. How I ever thought it would be anything else is beyond me. It was probably the proverbial military Kool-Aid I drank while I was in my early 20's and watching the Military Channel nonstop. I'd get to throw grenades, shoot cool weapons, camp, and work out all day. Yeah, I'd get yelled at, whatever, sign me up Mr. Recruiter guy in an office above a Burger King in Denton, Texas. Let's do this.

MEPS (Military Entrance Processing Station) is a place where EVERY single person hoping to join the Armed Forces is required to go to sign all of their paperwork. While you're there you take a physical, a drug test, and finally raise your right hand and swear to "support and defend the Constitution of the United States against all enemies, foreign and domestic." Unofficially, it's where you first forget the whole truth (lie) on government paperwork. They also make you strip down to your underwear in a room full of other people and waddle around like a duck. After that fun, they tell you to strip buck naked and bend over in front of an 80-year-old man (if you've been to the Dallas MEPS, you know the one). Oh, and don't forget to cough while you are spread eagle. MEPS smells like feet and crushed dreams for a reason. They want to set the stage for your first taste of what the military is.

Now, when I say forget to tell the whole truth I don't mean flat-out lying to the government employee that's asking you questions. No, no, no, someone of such high moral values wanting to serve their country in the military would NEEEEEVER. Just fucking kidding, we're all a bunch of scumbags that lied to get our way in. Remember most of us thought we were going to be Captain America, so we were willing to do anything to reach that goal. Before you get on your high horse, relax, Captain America probably lied too. That whole not telling the whole truth thing (what is the truth anyways?) begins with the recruiter. You know, the recruiter who gave you the Captain America speech while you ate your Burger King French fries. Those recruiters' sole job is to hit their numbers for the month. Army, Air Force, Marines, Navy, or Coast Guard, all of them. The top military officers need a certain number of people in their ranks and the recruiters are going to get them those people, at all costs. The slight majority of the demographic that the recruiters are dealing with that end up in the military may or may not have an arrest, drug use, nor meet the minimal requirements from the military to be able to join.

If you've ever seen the movie, *Get Hard* with Will Ferrell and Kevin Hart; military recruits are Will Ferrell and recruiters are Kevin Hart. If you haven't seen it, don't worry: Will Ferrell is a normal everyday guy that gets sentenced to prison for fraud and is given a month to get his affairs in order before going into prison. He hires Kevin Hart to prepare him for life inside prison; essentially to make him a hard ass. Hilarity ensues because Ferrell is a softy that is living a sheltered life in high-class suburbia and is naive to the real world. Kevin Hart comes in and gives him a dose of reality, teaches him some shit, and sends him on his way at the end (no spoilers). Well, recruiters' relationships with civilians look just like this. It is their job to take the guy smoking blunts and shot gunning Natty Lites and turn them into a presentable recruit.

No amount of books or YouTube videos will ever prepare you for the debauchery that is MEPS and basic training. That's why your recruiter is like your sensei. They are there to guide you through the poop river that is signing up for the military; on a canoe made of white lies and cigarettes. Recruiters take completely inept people off the streets and make sure they know when and where to lie and provide them the tools to carry out the lie. They get all of their paperwork together, then act as bail bondsmen who physically drive and walk the recruits into MEPS. They make sure that you have no way out of signing your life away. They watch you do the whole swearing-in thing and then you will never see them again (hopefully).

Now join me on the shit river boat that's held together by failed Special Forces contracts and orange juice. It all starts the night before you're set to go to your big day at MEPS. The military typically has a contract with a nearby hotel, so they put you up the night before where everybody going to MEPS the next day has to stay, even if you live right next door. The lack of trust. There are recruits from every branch of the military crammed into this hotel. None of them can be trusted to walk across the street, let alone get some place by themselves. They're driven by the recruiter and walked straight into the hotel where we will stay until morning, well at least where you are supposed to stay until morning. I'll get first-hand experience with that soon enough. In our hotel, the military had taken over 2 floors just for recruits. No need to check in at the front desk. The warden, I mean Sargent, has your key ready for you. I walked up the third floor to check in, get my room key, and itinerary for the day. Oh, and you give them your driver's license, you know, the whole trust thing. Pretty sure that's the first step in human trafficking but hey, it's the military, so shut up and do what we say.

I was given some simple ground rules from the check-in people: no booze, don't leave the hotel grounds, no member of the opposite sex in your room, in your room with lights out by 10 p.m. While being told this, I kept wondering who would do any of those things. I didn't join the military for a vacation. I joined to be Captain America. I quickly learned that lots of people would do these things, including Jessie. I grab my room key, hand over my license, and head up to my room: 527. Lucky for me, 527's air conditioning was broken. I walked into a musky and dirty room with a sweet ACU patterned digital camo backpack sitting on one of the queen beds. Damn, his recruiter hooked him up; I wish mine had too. Room 527 was my first experience with the foot and BO smell. It smelled like America . . . and a locker room.

I set my bag down before going into the dimly lit bathroom. I splash some water on my face and throw some more old spice under the pits (this tradition will quickly become my morning routine for my entire time in the Army). I was already sweating through the whole process, and we hadn't even done anything. It was around 1800 (or 6 p.m. for you civilian newbs) and my plan was to lay around and study my military rank structure (DORK). See, I was already basically in the Army, laying around in a non-airconditioned room, wearing Old Spice, and using the military vernacular. This shit's gonna be a breeze. About the time I had memorized my way up to the rank of Colonel (not pronounced how it's spelled, thanks Obama), the door opens and in walks Jessie. He is the living and breathing definition of a small-town boy. I would have been shocked if he had ever seen an elevator floor count go above 3. He must have been a straight out of high school type of recruit. Now, I grew up in a small town but there are levels to this shit and he was on another one than me.

"Oh, what's up man, I'm Jessie. I guess we're roommates now," he introduced himself with a hearty handshake.

"Nice to meet you, roomie, I'm Brian."

"The AC is broke, but whatever, this place is nice init??"

"Uhhhh yeah man it's great." I replied.

Trying to make conversation and connect with what I thought would be a like-minded future troop, I ask, "Wanna go get some chow (dinner, for you civilians) downstairs? It's free." Jessie's response is where I first started to realize the melting pot that is the military. Before his answer, I thought that at least everyone was on the same page about why we were in this 1.69-star hotel. I came to take care of business and start my long journey to being a service member. It seemed Jessie came for another reason; I just wasn't sure what that reason was yet.

"Nah man I'm good, I've been drinkin' beers behind that Shell across the street with TJ from the fourth floor." There's his reason.

I'VE BEEN DRINKIN' BEERS BEHIND THAT SHELL ACROSS THE STREET WITH TJ FROM THE FOURTH FLOOR.

I've been blessed with the ability to hold it together when somebody is telling me some wild shit. I looked back at him and said, "right on man, I'll be down there if you wanna come." As soon as I got into the hallway, I started whispering to myself in total disbelief. *Doesn't he know we get breathalyzed and drug tested tomorrow? What about the no booze rule? The whole no leaving the hotel grounds thing?* By this time, you are probably realizing just how big of a dork I really am. I am a rule follower. I joined the military in order to serve in the military. I quickly am realizing that I am the exception to the rule in this endeavor. I then start thinking about the trouble Jessie may get me into with his debauchery. *What if he tries to bring a girl back to our room? Oh, dear God, what if I get in trouble too?* Jessie had put my mind in a blender with his Natty Lite breath and I didn't know what to do next. My pits are definitely buggin' at this point and that second layer of Old Spice was gone before I even got down to the cold mashed potatoes set up in a conference room downstairs. In my mind I was already roughing it by eating them, but boy oh boy was I in for a treat. I finished chow, grabbed a banana for a little snack later then headed back up to 527 with the hopes of watching a nice movie and bonding with Jessie before falling asleep around 2200 (10 p.m., newbs).

As I came up to my door, I heard some talking coming from 527. *Oh jeez, is Jessie's drinkin' buddy TJ in there?* Again, sweat poured from my pits. My anxiety was going through the black-mold-havin' roof. I put my key in and open it up to find a guy in uniform standing right in the middle of our room. This guy was giving ole Jessie the straight business. I see myself as a cultured man when it comes to fuckery and even I was surprised by some of the four-letter adjective combinations this mysterious man was able to put together. Mainly, I stood in that doorway thinking my time in the Army was already up. My rule-following self was already spiraling into thinking that Jessie was implicating me. Was he telling this guy that I was in on his little drink behind the fucking gas station across from a shitty hotel plan? Now I could feel the sweat/Old Spice combo dripping down my side like the fountain of anxiety it was. What felt like at least 69 minutes standing in that doorway watching my life flash before my eyes was in reality only about 10 seconds, I finally had gathered enough courage to step inside the room and casually say, "oh hey, how's it going?" *Why was my voice squeaky like I'm 12? What a dork.*

"I'm Jessie's recruiter, we're just handling some business. You don't have anything to worry about," was the guy's response. He said it in a way that made it clear that shit was about to go down in that musky room. That recruiter looked at me in a way that said *don't even think about saying shit about fuck of what's going on in this shitty room right now.* I just nodded, sat down in the dirty chair in the corner, and tried to blend right into the wall. I must have done a really good job of turning into that wall because they went about their business like I was not even there. Like a true bro, the recruiter goes over to his backpack behind the door and says, "dude I told you, you have to get drug tested and breathalyzed tomorrow." He is getting more angry when he continues to say, "why you gotta be smokin' weed and drinking fucking beer the day before you go to MEPS?" *Oh my god! Did I hear that right? Excuse me, sir did you say SMOKING WEED AND DRINKING BEER?*

I was about to have a heart attack and stroke out over in that nasty-ass chair. *Was Jessie about to get court martialed right before my eyes? What the fuck is going on here? Why am I not even officially in the Army yet and dudes are already acting a fool smoking weed by the dumpster in a Shell parking lot across the street from a military hotel?* I was so ready to blurt out, "I WASN'T THERE I DIDN'T DO ANYTHING!" But deep down, it kind of excited me to be a part of this. It was like knowing you're a part of something bad. It was like when you catch yourself rooting for the bad guy and secretly want to be a part of their street gang. That's how I already started to feel and I wasn't even in the Army yet! Ohh boy.

What happened next in room 527 would become one of the biggest lessons I learned in the Army. That recruiter, even being as mad as he was, took care of Jessie. Straightened someone out so nobody would get in trouble from higher command. What that recruiter did would stick with me and is going to be a continuous theme throughout this book: no matter how shitty the circumstances we're in, we can still have each other's back. We hear it all the time from people that have seen combat, "no matter what, I wanted to have the guy's back that was next to me." It doesn't matter if you hated that person. When the shit is hitting the fan, you come together. For the longest time, I never understood that.

I told myself that I needed to be in combat with bullets flying past and bombs going off to feel that connection, but now I see that's not the case at all. I had formed a bond and connection that I didn't even know was possible in humans; right there in wonderful hotel room #527.

Back to that room and how the recruiter took care of Jessie. He goes and grabs his backpack he had brought in from behind the door and sets it on the bed. He pulls out a gallon jug of water and a small box that looks like Jell-O powder mix. Then he tells Jessie, "Pour this whole box of gelatin in that gallon jug and drink it until it's gone." He continued his instructions by including, "you can't go to bed before you drink it. I don't care if you don't sleep. It's going to clear out your system before tomorrow." The recruiter describes how Jessie will piss it all out and be good to go for his drug test. Wow. I'm pretty sure I was just an accomplice to a felony but, whatever, I'm in it to win it now. The rest of the night goes off without a hitch. Jessie stays up drinking his gelatin water and I toss and turn all night because it's damp and smelly. It may have also been the anxiety of signing my life away the next day (well as long as the butthole doctor says it's okay).

The next morning, I wake up to a phone call from the front desk as an alarm because again, none of us can be trusted; as Jessie has proven. I ask Jessie how he's feeling, and he says "waterlogged, but fine" Jessie quickly says goodbye once we get downstairs to the cafeteria and runs over to his boy TJ. They have a degenerate reunion and run off to eat together. My recruiter is there and gathers the group of us that came together so he can tell us not to drink the orange juice. He is worried it will spike our heart rate and maybe make us fail the physical. Pretty sure there's no science behind that but I didn't ask for the peer-reviewed study. I just nodded my head and went for the ice water instead, safety first. As I'm standing in line to load up my plate with some nice, powdered eggs, I get to hear a mind-boggling conversation going on between two dudes in front of me. One guy apparently has just found out via the other gentlemen that his "SEAL" contract does NOT actually guarantee that he will become a NAVY SEAL. As a cherry on top, the other guy tells him and that if he fails out of BUD/S he will be forced into whatever job the big Navy needs. The normal Navy with the peasants. He turned ghostly white and scuttled off to a table to pick at his powder eggs and contemplate the meaning of life. I have often wondered what happened to him. That quickly reminded me that recruiters will definitely forget to tell you some stuff if it gets you to sign your life away. How many 18-year-olds were told "oh yeah bro I got you signed up to be a SEAL, no problemo" just to end up peeling potatoes in the bottom of a submarine somewhere (no offense to cooks). All good, I'm ready to get this party going. Let's get my butthole checked, sign on the dotted line, and become a soldier. HOOOOAHHH!

Before we all pile onto buses headed for the MEPS building, my recruiter rounds up the ten or so of us one last time and gives us a pep talk that sums up MEPS as a whole: "Congratulations, you're all Superman for the day. You've never had a broken bone, never needed stitches, never been in a car accident, and never so much as gotten a parking ticket." He even made us repeat it to him . . . "I am Superman for the day, I've never had stitches . . ."

Alrighty then, this whole forgetting to tell the whole truth thing is off to a hot start. I'm ready to do this thing. Unlike what it may have read like, all of that stuff above happened in less than 24 hours and now we finally find ourselves standing outside the MEPS building. We're waiting in line like it's the release of the latest PlayStation at Best Buy and we are trying to get our hands on one. Everyone is told to shut up by a mean-looking gentleman in a uniform and then given some basic instructions before the doors open. You go through some metal detectors and start piling into an elevator that smells like…you guessed it…feet and BO. My pits are dripping before the doors even open. Once the doors finally open, all you can see if a big open space with cubicles, offices, conference-looking rooms, a cafeteria, and a sitting area. At least the sitting area had an old-school big-screen TV with the Military Channel playing 24/7.

The energy in that room was a mix of excitement, uncertainty, and disappointment. For some people they were fulfilling lifelong dreams by joining but for others they would be denied the opportunity to enlist and end up rejected by the military. Anytime there was a group of us gathered around, unverified rumors were flying around. We wondered how long we were going to have to be there? Would lunch be served? Were we supposed to bring lunch? Was a certain military branch was even taking people that day? What is the physical going to be like? The physical was a big one. Nervousness about failing it was palpable and you could have cut the anxiety of failing it with a cold butter knife. You would have thought that we were having to complete an Ironman triathlon to be able to enlist.

After sitting around, watching the TV from the '90s, and gathering false information, my name and number are finally called. Time to mount up and spring into action. I'm put into a group of about 20 recruits where we continue to wait. We were moved outside a double door that leads us into step one of the physical. Quickly, the guy in charge pulls out a breathalyzer and I can physically see people's faces drop to the ground. The Jessies of the group that had probably drank beers behind whatever gas station in whatever town next to whatever shitty hotel the military put them up in were now ghost white. Mouths wide open. Maybe we should have believed the recruiters when they said you were going to be doing this exact thing, huh fellas? In any case, I was there for the entertainment and to see their dreams being crushed right before my eyes. I was not even in the Army yet and was seeing people get kicked out right in front of me. You never forget your first time, right?

It took 3 or 4 people, but that breathalyzer finally sniped its first victim that was standing out right in the open with a target right on its back. Might as well have been holding a sign saying, "shoot here." Mind you, this breathalyzer wasn't to see if you were even at the .08 legal limit to drive, it was trying to see if you had ANY alcohol in your system. As in you need to blow .00 even to be let into the room to actually begin your physical. The first victim blew like a .01 or something. His head hung so low it's practically detached from his head. The guy in charge of administering the test just calmly explains to him that he can't move any further into today's tests and needs to call his recruiter to come pick him up. Wonder what that guy was thinking whenever he failed the breathalyzer? Was he one of the ones that were promised to become a Navy SEAL and were just out celebrating with some Natty Lites with the boys or what? Or was he from a really small town with very little money and got to go to the "big city" for the first time in his life and got carried away by the bright lights? Either way, I felt for the dude but still giggled to myself and filled the space left by him in the line. That breathalyzer was the grim reaper for another 3 victims out of our group. This brought our attrition rate to 25% and we hadn't even done anything but breathed into a machine yet. Saddle up everyone, we're in for a long day at this rate.

The double doors open, and I walk into what can only be described as an open room that's a mix between an exam room and a conference room. The floors were bare and various metal cabinets were along the wall at random intervals. The smell was an interesting mix of bleach, ripe butthole that probably needs to be wiped, sweaty feet, and Axe body spray. We were all told to go to one side of the large square room and strip down to our underwear. Ohhhh, so that's where the butthole, foot, and Axe body spray smell was coming from. Everyone's bare ass and feet had just been out in this room all day.

Once a group was done, and this is a wild guess, the people that work there probably just spray Lysol Disinfectant straight into the air. FYI, the Axe that everyone sprayed to cover up their BO is stronger than that Lysol pal. It should be noted here that this room's air conditioning wasn't set to a cool 70 degrees; it was probably 80 degrees there. My armpits are dripping sweat straight down my side at this point, no doubt contributing to the smell.

I'm just awkwardly standing there with all the other dudes in their boxers. The military is a big melting pot, but at the end of the day we are all just sweaty feet, buttholes, and Axe body spray. Then we were split into two lines and essentially told to put on a naked fashion runway show for the "evaluator." They had us walk normally, then on our tiptoes, then backwards on our tiptoes, then on our heels, then sideways. Then, the coup de gras: the dreaded duck walk. The duck walk has wreaked havoc in military recruit circles for decades, ruining many a chance for joining the military. It was everywhere in the military message boards at the time (yes, we had those in 2008). I had practiced it and knew it was hard but was definitely still nervous because that evaluator in the room is the ultimate decider. If they decided your duck walk looked like kaka then you went home for the day to . . . go get better knees and try again later I guess???

So, what is a duck walk? Definitely type in "Duck Walk MEPS" on YouTube but I'm going to do my best to describe it. Feel free to have a giggle at my attempt to describe this. Here goes. You start at the very bottom of a squat on your tiptoes, then move forward in a heel-to-toe pattern while holding the bottom of the squat position. And not the bottom of a Planet Fitness squat, the pickup a blade of freshly cut grass with your ass cheeks bottom of a squat. Boy, oh boy, the cracking in that room was echoing off the sterile floors and metal cabinets. Not to mention the muffled moans and groans as we were all trying to mask the fact that it was painful and hard. A couple of people just couldn't even get that low but were forced to keep trying the entire time down and back, about 15 yards or so. I made it through without the evaluator putting a big red Sharpie line through the first form in my packet, while others weren't so lucky and got the red line of death. The red line of death meant you had to go sit out in the waiting room and call their recruiter to tell them they failed the duck walk. It was starting to seem like that call back to your recruiter was going to be worse than calling mom and dad after you'd been picked up by the cops for being drunk in public. Sheesh. As we were all getting dressed, the evaluator announced the shocking revelation that it smelled like shit in his room and to get out immediately. Oh, really dude, we were the first group that smelled like FAA (feet, ass, Axe)?! I'm sure.

Whatever, back to watching the Military Channel and having anxiety about what's next. After another 2 hours or so, my name is called again from the pulpit. I was put into another group of a dozen or so and shuttled down a hallway into a waiting area. Surprisingly, there were no magazines to thumb through. This time, we were all given a little speech on how to take a urinalysis. They gave us cups with our names and social security numbers printed on the label and told to line up against the wall. The rules sounded very serious. The Cliffs Note version: groups of three will go into the bathroom, line up on a spot in the trough, drop their pants AND underwear to their ankles, and lastly hold your left hand over their head with the cup in the right hand. *Seems oddly specific but got it.* The guys in uniform checked out everyone's private parts to make sure no funny business was going on. Then they gave the signal to begin, and you are expected to begin urinating. They say to piss into the metal trough, then into *your* (this was emphasized for some reason??) cup until there is urine past the line. When the looker says you're good, you put the lid on, pull your pants up, and exit the room. By the way, "the looker" is standing directly in front of the trough looking at everyone with their pants at their ankles taking a leak. Talk about stage fright. I was downing water all day to prepare for this, so I was obviously the first one done. On my way out I heard grumblings from the last guy left in my trough group about how he couldn't pee and that he was nervous. The looker said, "don't care, I can stand here all day," and went back to looking directly at his junk without batting an eye. I bet the looker had seen it all: small bottles of clean pee smuggled in, stuff smuggled up the butt, chemicals on the hand, etc. Anything you can think of, he had probably seen in that pink-tiled room with a horse trough as a urinal. Wonder how Jessie was doing during this phase? Was he sweatin' it or was he confident in his gelatin/gallon of water combo? By the way, I have no clue if that combo works, so don't try it then blame me if you still fail a drug test.

We were sent back to the little waiting area in the hallway outside the bathroom door and were left to worry about what was to come next. I had a good idea of what it was and still trying to think of ways to get out of it. I was pretty sure it was time to bend over and show that butthole to an old man, but I was also getting hungry, so my mind was in a blender. I spent the next 30 painstaking minutes trying to block out the fact that I had to expose my sweaty, stinky, anxiety-ridden body to yet another stranger today. Eventually, a very nice young nurse came out of an 8-by-8 exam room and told me to have a seat inside. Just like any other checkup visit to the doctor growing up, she took my blood pressure, checked my pulse, looked in my ears and eyes, felt my back while I coughed, all that normal stuff.

Then . . . THEN . . . there he was. In the flesh, the old man himself. The one whose reputation has preceded him and the one who I know will be staring directly into my soul via my butthole. This part of the physical was the hands-on part. I was nervous and anxious about it to say the least. I might as well not even had deodorant on at this point, it was long gone. Nonetheless, the old man doctor guy introduces himself and I promptly forget his name. I'm too busy worrying about if he's going to tell me to go sit down and call my recruiter because I have an ugly butthole. But I manage to get up out of that seat and make the slow walk down the hall into this office.

I could see the looks of despair and concern on the faces of the other recruits lined up in that hallway as I walked by. They bowed their heads and I'm pretty sure I heard someone grumble "dead man walking." My feet are heavy and start to shuffle and the 6-second walk to get there felt like 6 hours. Of course, this old man doctor who has been giving military recruits physicals for decades wanted to make small talk. And of course, he has a second cousin that has passed through the small town I grew up in. I wanted so badly to just drop my pants and yell "HERE IT IS, NOW LOOK AT IT AND LET'S MOVE ON." But I didn't, I stayed strong. I let him finish talking and watched in horror as he snapped his latex gloves on. Just as you'd imagine. I half excitedly hopped down and started undressing like it was prom night, but the old man doctor guy told me no, no, not yet. Alright, fine. He goes through my reflexes, ears, and eyes; you know the stuff his nurse did no less than 10 minutes ago. Then he says the thing . . . go ahead and drop your pants and underwear to your ankles. Thank God. Let's get this over with.

Let's take a second to remember that rumors were floating around from survivors that he sticks a finger up your butthole. Some people swore that it happened while others swore that it didn't. Either way, there was only one way to find out. First up is the hernia check which happens in the testicles while you're coughing . . . and "again". "Okay, looks good," Pause. Paaaaaause. *Wait am I about to get out of having to turn around and show him my...* "Okay, go ahead and turn around, bend over, and spread your butt cheeks." Nope, there it is. I turned around, bent over, and spread my butt cheeks to show this old man doctor what I'm workin with. He looked at it for a quick second, snapped his gloves off, and said, "Okay, you're all good." It's so vile for me to even type that, but it's the truth. I'm sure it stunk. I'm sure everyone's stunk and has stunk for the past 40 years this guy's been checking buttholes. My pants go back on with a swiftness. He signs off on my chart, hands it back, and says he'll look me up next time he's in Whitesboro. Please don't, but okay bye. Whew, what a relief, the physical part of my time at MEPS is done and now I just have to sit around and do nothing while the mountain of paperwork required to enlist gets straightened out. Then I swear in.

The paperwork part is pretty uneventful other than the fact that I felt obligated to read the important parts like how long I'm property of the government, what my job is going to be, and the dates I enter and exit. Ya know, responsible stuff. I will say trying to read over the no kidding 100 pages of government-type documents can start to feel like you are reading the terms and conditions on Facebook. So I was looking for dates, my name, and words like "forfeit" and "rights." Those seemed important.

After only misspelling my name once and having to wait in the main lobby for another hour while they fixed it, I was finally ready to sign my life away. It's quite uneventful and definitely not like the movies. There was no dramatic signing of a scroll in a picturesque town square with bald eagles overhead and bombs bursting in the air. Maybe I had hyped myself up too much because it was a cubicle with a desktop computer and a man highlighting the important parts and ensuring I understood what my signature meant. I think we all think we know what it means, but really, we don't. An hour later after I raised my right hand and swore my allegiance to the constitution I was officially in the Army. Damn, what do I do now?

CHAPTER 2: SHARK ATTACK

squinting "Is that a . . . No, no way that's a . . ."

–Every new recruit looking at the contraband board

I still had 2 months from the time I swore into the time I actually left for basic training. So, to answer my own question from the end of the last chapter: I sell all of my belongings, go to Las Vegas to party for New Year's, and overdraft my bank account of course. New year, new me, ya know?

[Real quick, I apologize for the number of times we talked about buttholes in the last chapter. It had to be done. I needed you to be in that room with me, to smell the smell of those rooms through the pages. But it's over, for now. Until we have to check each other's buttholes for ticks later on. But hey, that's it, I promise!]

This was 2008, headed into 2009, so a pretty big part of me knew that there was more than a good chance that I was going to be sent off to Iraq or Afghanistan to fight in a war. The possibility of not coming back the same, if at all, was there but I never gave it much thought. That sounds dramatic now considering that I was ultimately sent to a non-deployable unit and would never fire my service weapon anywhere other than a range but it's definitely how I felt going into basic training.

But on February 19, 2009, my friend dropped me off at the recruiting station (the one next to the Burger King) and I hopped in my recruiter's car on one last ride to MEPS. I had my super hooah Digi Camo backpack with the Go Army logo on it, a 50-dollar bill (thanks mom!), all of my paperwork I had signed at MEPS earlier, a one-way airline ticket, and a temporary military ID with my name spelled wrong on it. Awesome. Off to a great start. Of course, the shitty old bus that's transporting about 20 of us to the airport so we can catch our appropriate flights breaks down 5 minutes into the 30-minute commute. You could taste the cumulative anxiety of all 20 of us that we were going to miss our flights to basic training and be completely fucked. It tasted like old Skittles and pickle juice in there. Wouldn't ya know it, my shirt was drenched in sweat. Thanks for nothin' again, Old Spice. A backup bus comes, and we make it to the airport on time.

I met up with a couple of other dudes headed to Ft. Leonardwood and we start dishing about our anxieties and the rumors we had heard of; mainly how bad it was going to be. After three layovers and zero adult supervision, I finally made it on a bus headed to Ft. Leonardwood, Missouri. It was 11 p.m. and you could have heard a pin drop in that bus the entire drive. I positioned myself in the back of the bus just in case drill sergeants came on board and started punching the first people they saw in the face. In my head it was a good possibility that they step on the bus like it's the middle of a Slipknot mosh pit. We had all succumbed to our fates and realized we had zero control over what happened with our lives once this bus stopped.

After an hour's trip in the pitch-black darkness of night, we rolled into the main gate of Ft. Leonardwood -my home for the next 5 months. As we're starting to wind our way through Ft. Leonardwood to the in-processing buildings we all start to get nervous. We had all seen on the recruiting videos and movies that this is about where the verbal onslaught by drill sergeants begins. The ones where spit is flying everywhere, words that you can't even understand are being yelled at you, you're fumbling with your bag, and your shoe is untied. You try tying it and get yelled at even more because you're now playing a game of Simon Says but basically in a different language. There's a name for these types of onslaughts, "Shark Attacks". I remember my first time. It was anticlimactic and was over before I knew it. Just like my other first time, you know the one. My first encounter with a drill sergeant was with a very tired one at midnight on a smelly bus full of dehydrated, anxiety-ridden recruits. Much to my dismay, it wasn't a swarm of great whites but rather a tired leopard shark. The ones that are completely harmless to humans.

The airbrakes let out in front of a building, and we all hold our breaths for what's to come next, pretty sure somebody even threw a Hail Mary out there. Then it happened: he stepped on the bus and yelled out, "asses down, eyes on me". Fear, panic, and anxiety abound. Some had never been yelled at before and their ghostly faces wore it most. After those initial five words of yelling this leopard shark drill sergeant slowly and calmly explains to us what we need to do next. He was definitely tired, so he didn't have the energy to give us full great white shark energy. You could tell he clearly wanted to be done with us so he could go home and probably drink an ice-cold beer. We needed to grab our bags, put them in our right hand, and line up on the yellow line right outside the bus. He would tell us what to do next once we all got out there. So, we do what he says with a lot of bags being fumbled in wonderment of which hand is our right hand. Eventually, we're all standing on that yellow line. Damn, it's cold out here. There's snow on the ground and it's pitch black. Here. We. Go. 'Ole leopard shark drill sergeant goes on to tell us that we're at the in-processing building for Ft. Leonardwood. He continues to tell us that this is where we're going to be living for the next couple of weeks while we get our shots and all of our paperwork in line. After that, we will be shipped off to our actual basic training unit.

"But first things first," the leopard shark drill sergeant says, "I'm going to open this door and you're going to go find a table in the room in front of you. Set your backpack on that table and hold your ID in your right hand. Then stand there until my friends come into the room. We are going to search all of your bags for contraband". Seems simple enough I thought. Surely nobody would actually smuggle something in. Quickly, I was brought down to reality by the reminder of my roommate, Jessie at MEPS, and how he drank beer and smoked weed the day before we were supposed to swear into the military. *We're a band of dirtbags.* Sure enough, as I walked through that door there was a huge glass display of all the contraband that had been seized from dirt bag recruits that had come before me. One of the tiger shark drill sergeant's friends appeared and started giving us a loud speech. He went over what wasn't allowed and how they have to search our bags and yell at us because we can't be trusted.

"Privates (a rank that everyone is called during basic training) just like you have tried to smuggle in all of the stuff you see in that display, so I don't trust any of you for shit." *From my experience so far, you shouldn't actually trust any of us, so fair game drill sergeant lady, search away. I want to see if any of the other people are trying to smuggle in some cigs or something anyways.*

The drill sergeants that were doing all the searching at those tables were loud and more like what I had expected drill sergeants to be, but I remember getting the vibe that they were more annoyed by us then we were by them. They were obviously annoyed by our smelly existence and the fact they had to be up at midnight with us more than anything else. It's like when you're a teenager and your 10-year-old younger brother and his friends are cluelessly harassing you. The drill sergeants were the teenagers and us smelly privates were the 10-year-olds. They were seemingly playing characters and trolling us along the way. As they're searching through everyone's stuff that is laid out on the table, they're throwing unnecessary stuff over their shoulders then yelling at you to pack it all back up. And hurry. I guess I didn't need my Blockbuster card from my wallet anymore after all.

After all my belongings got searched, I couldn't take my eyes off that glass display box of all the stuff people have tried to smuggle in. It was a reminder of why silly, super-detailed rules are rules. Someone had actually tried to smuggle a dildo into basic training. That's why. Here are some of the things from that glorious glass box: a compact pistol; various-sized knives; fireworks (M-80's looked to be most popular); smoke bombs; condoms; a cell phone; rope; and a big, glorious, pink dildo parked front and center.

After we all made it through the search and were holding our bags, the drill sergeants left and we all stood there for another 30 minutes. It was my first experience with the classic "hurry up and wait" modality. This particular modality turned into an omen as to what the military is and would become for me: standing around and waiting on nothing. About when my legs were falling asleep and I couldn't shift my weight around any longer, we were told to stand in line in an adjacent hallway "nuts to butts". Nuts to butts? "Yeah, exactly what it means privates. I want you so close to the person in front of you that *your* nuts are on *their* butts." Remember the smell I talked about earlier? Standing in that hallway, I got to experience it up close and personal with my newfound comrades. After another 10 minutes of standing nuts to butts, we were finally shuttled into a huge, open room with bunk beds all around and told to find an empty spot.

"When the lights come on in the morning, get up and follow everyone else. They'll know what to do."

Reminder, it's about 2 a.m. at this point, pitch black, everyone is asleep, and I have no idea where I'm at. I weave my way through the dozens of bunk beds and finally find a top bunk in the back corner by the bathroom. I climb up and lay down on a bare mattress with my backpack as a pillow and fall asleep after about 20 minutes of worrying about if I'm in the right spot. *Do the people in charge know that I'm here? Is this the right building? What if they're out looking for me and I'm not there? and, and, and . . .* I get what feels like 20 minutes of sleep that first night when the lights come on and everyone wakes up. There's at least a hundred of us in that room and I look down and meet my bunkmate who tells me to go to the bathroom, wash my face, and brush my teeth. He then says, "then we'll go out to formation and get broken into groups to go do other stuff". He had a uniform on and I was still in my clothes from the day before. *Was I supposed to have a uniform on? I don't know, fuuuuuuck!*

That first morning at breakfast was very anticlimactic: no yelling, no hurrying to eat, I ate some Oreos. It was nothing like what I was expecting. The guys around me that had been there longer than me quickly reminded me that this was nothing like actual basic training and that these drill sergeants just needed to keep us alive and shuttle us around.

And that was basically the routine for the next 2 weeks: sleep in the big open room, wake up, brush your teeth, eat breakfast, get broken into groups at morning formation, then go get all the things you were going to need to actually go to your basic training unit and start training. There wasn't a lot of yelling, but a ton of nuts to butts waiting around—hurrying up and waiting.

Mondays and Thursdays we changed our sheets. The area to drop off and pick up new sheets was also the area where suicide watch was also happening. It threw me off guard, we weren't even doing basic training stuff yet but a guy was standing outside of a dark room with no boot laces or belt. Turns out he was having problems with his paperwork and physical. He had been in-processing for a month and was having a tough time living in purgatory.

One thing you do learn during in-processing is how to stay awake when you literally have nothing to do. As I said, there was lots of waiting around doing nothing during this phase. At the same time, you weren't allowed to sleep, to have caffeine, or to talk to anyone. The most terrible version of a meditation practice This is where I was introduced to the powerful drug that is hand sanitizer. We were all issued a bottle of it, "because y'all are nasty privates". Boy, oh boy, had I never seen hand sanitizer be used in the way that people were using it: smelling it, licking it, putting a couple drops in the mouth, actually snorting it, applying it as under the eye moisturizer, using it as eye drops. It was being used in any way to harness the power of the rubbing alcohol to help stay awake. The underground king of performance-enhancing drugs. It would continue to play a role in keeping us all awake for the next 5 months. But like most good drugs, you built up a tolerance to it. So eventually it required more sniffs and licks to get the rush you once did at the beginning. Don't judge, I blame it on big pharma, getting us all hooked on hand sanitizer and all. I'm proud to report I've been clean and sober from it since the day I left Ft. Leonardwood. There should be a challenge coin for that or something.

The place was starting to feel like a prison. Not in the way of not being able to leave or feeling like I was being punished for some egregious wrong I had committed against society as a whole. Well, now that I type that last sentence it did feel like those things too. You definitely couldn't just walk out, and head home and you were definitely being punished for something you did wrong. You could get punished for something as small as walking wrong. It mainly felt like a prison because of the underground culture that I was starting to notice and be a part of. There were boundaries, both physically and mentally, put in place by drill sergeants to keep us all wrangled up and in line.

Some people had been in in-processing longer than me and they definitely knew the ins and outs of the place. They knew how to live in the gray and knew how to get away with some stuff without getting in trouble. They were the OGs that we all aspired to be in a weird way. They were fearless, it seemed, and they were the people who showed us new people how to snort hand sanitizer. I imagine it's basically the same thing as prison: OG's showing the young bucks a thing or two on how to survive. One distinct way of telling an OG apart from everyone else was that they had actually been issued their uniforms and name tapes. It took about a week to be issued your uniform, boots, and an actual name tape (name badge). That means that at any given time there was a mix of people wearing Army uniforms and people wearing regular clothes off the streets. A band of misfits to say the least. A band that sniffs hand sanitizer to stay awake. Sheesh, name that street gang. Once you were wearing your uniform, you de facto became an OG. You had the unspoken responsibility of teaching the newbs how to survive. Dirtbags taking care of their own.

Let's talk about penicillin shots and why they were the most feared things during that in-processing time. A big part of everyone's in-processing into the military basically getting sterilized and ridden of all of our germs both externally and internally. I definitely don't know all the shots I was given during that time (or during my time as a whole in the Army) and the environment wasn't exactly conducive to questioning it either. We were told to line up, roll our right sleeves up, and step forward when it was our turn. The government was in control now and everyone had accepted their fates at that point, so we rolled up our sleeves and got stuck with probably five different needles. Then we walked into the next room and the panic really started to set in. The penicillin shot was called the peanut butter shot because it felt like a lump of peanut butter was slammed directly into the side of your butt cheek. It stayed there for a few days at least; so, nobody was extra excited about having a peanut butter ass to say the least. The arm shots were no big deal, but peanut butter butt? That's a "no" from everyone.

From an actual medical sense, the peanut butter butt shot is an antibiotic that is used to treat and prevent certain bacterial infections. In military terms, it's a cheap, easy, and semi-effective way to try to keep a large group of people from spreading nasty sicknesses to each other. Luckily for me, my mom had told me once that they thought that I was maybe, possibly I was allergic to penicillin when I was a baby, but who knows if I am now. Say less, mom.

I walked into the room where peanut butter butts are made with all my medical paperwork from MEPS saying that I was healthy as a horse. You could cut the anxiety in that room with a cold butter knife. Everyone's faces were drawn in with eyes on the ground; fates were sealed. We were all going to be getting peanut butter shots in a matter of minutes. Then it happens, a wave of courage I've never felt before overtakes me like a hurricane. I step up to the nurse that is taking everyone's medical charts who is prepping the syringe of the thick substance that is definitely too thick to be going into anyone's buttocks. As my outstretched arm is about to reach hers, I blurt out, "MY PAPERWORK IS MESSED UP, I'M ACTUALLY ALLERGIC TO PENICILLIN."

My heart was pounding and I felt like Ralphie from *A Christmas Story*. The part when Santa kicks him down the slide but he stops himself before blurting out he wants a Red Rider BB gun. I wanted to not have peanut butter butt for a week just like Ralphie wanted that BB gun, so I threw out a Hail Mary. It was later in the afternoon and this nurse that was on the receiving end of my Hail Mary had clearly had enough of smelly, snotty kids standing in front of her all day. She rolled her eyes so hard I swear they got stuck in the top of her head for a second. She then let out an audible sigh and said, "Oh reaaaaallllly?" I immediately said, "yes ma'am" and gave my best halfway nervous smile to her. Another eye roll, this time they get stuck at the bottom, and she stamps a big red stamp on my paperwork and tells me to go to the next room. Did I just pull off a miracle? I feel like a million bucks and couldn't believe I didn't have to get peanut butter stuck in my ass like these other poor schmucks around here. See ya later losers, we pure bloods got stuff to do.

More nuts to butts standing around, other random paperwork like getting to "pick out" where you want to be stationed (I'm sure). Surprisingly, I was in the minority when I picked out the most exotic places presented to me: Hawaii, Germany, and Italy. No offense to Kentucky but I didn't sign my life away to live there. One payphone call to home then a group of us got our names called and were told we were going to our actual basic training unit tomorrow. It was time to move on from gen pop, er, in-processing, and move into my cell block, er, basic training company.

Wonder and excitement were in the air after dinner that night. We were packing up all our stuff into our duffle bags to ship out the next day. We were the OGs that were leaving and passing on our underground knowledge to the younger generation of in-processing degenerates. It was time for us to start serving our real sentences, I mean actually start training to be soldiers.

After a restless night, a fresh shave, and a quick tutorial by a 40-year-old man on how to quickly throw your duffle bag on, we were all lined up outside in the freezing cold with our duffle bags. You guessed it, nuts to butts, waiting for our ride. Then, half a dozen trucks pulling cattle trailers pulled up and let off their air brakes. We were all looking around, wondering why they were going to be loading up a bunch of livestock right here, but whatever, the Army has been nothing but weird so far. That's when a whole gang of drill sergeants with their Smokey-the-Bear-looking hats jump out of the back of those cattle trailers and start yelling at the top of their lungs. I didn't know sharks could survive in the back of cattle trailers but sure enough, there they were. Now the real journey starts.

CHAPTER 3: TALES FROM THE TRAILER PARK

"Why don't you get down and beat your face, private?"

–Every Drill Sergeant ever

In case you didn't pick up on it, those cattle trailers were actually our rides to actual basic training. Our new home for the next 5 months. I wasn't expecting a luxury tour bus to come pick me up, but I definitely didn't expect to be sitting/standing in a livestock trailer either. Looking around, I got the feeling I wasn't the only one having those feelings but there was no time to think about it now. With our duffle bags on our chests, unable to see, we were literally corralled into the livestock trailers and told to bury our faces inside our duffle bags. Wouldn't want to let us see where we were headed in case we wanted to escape and all. Nonetheless, once inside, the drill sergeant assigned to be the cowboy wrangler of us human livestock was yelling to "Cram in more! More More! Squeeze in, squeeze in!" Then finally, "Just sit on top of them!" Sit on top of them?! Wait, am I going to a labor camp or a basic training unit here?

Then the moment happened that broke my fear and made me see the drill sergeants for what they were—humans just doing a job. Drill Sergeant VanStill was on my particular cattle truck, and she was standing on the railing that created the stalls inside the trailers. She was going back and forth, yelling at people to cram in tighter and tighter. On one of her balancing acts between railings, she stepped directly onto my head, bonking me like a whack-a-mole. Of course, I said nothing because I wasn't about to say shit about fuck to anyone at any time until I figured out what was what. I just figured that maybe that was part of the hazing phase of basic training—getting kicked in the head by a drill sergeant. I went about my own business of staring into the green duffle back that my face was on and thought nothing of it. We finally get what I would guess is 50 people inside the cattle trailer I was in and took off rumbling to God only knows where.

Once we got yelled at and told to keep our faces buried into that duffle bag, don't talk, don't breathe too loud, and barely blink; Drill Sergeant VanStill came from my blind side, bent down, and whispered in my ear. "Hey man, sorry for stepping on you earlier, you alright?" I nodded my head, and she was gone again, back to yelling at people on a cattle trailer in the middle of winter in Missouri. About 10 minutes later, our cattle truck finally stops and lets off its air brakes and it's go time. Before you know it, it's complete pandemonium. While running off the trailer trying to balance duffle bags on our chests, the Drill Sergeants are yelling numbers at us. They were yelling numbers one through four and expecting us to hear them clearly. Once we've run another 5 feet or so, you hear other voices yelling, "ONES OVER HERE, THREES OVER THERE, TWOS HERE, FOURS OVER THERE". I could see drill sergeants standing in front lines that were forming corresponding to that number.

AHHHHH, shit I forgot my number, so I half run, half waddle with a duffle bag on my chest over to line number three; cause why not? The cattle trucks roll out nice and slow to be sure we've gotten a good long look at our last hope for freedom, leaving us behind like scared baby calves to be slaughtered. Then we do what we've been trained so well to do already: we hurry up and wait. We are yelled at to have our faces plastered to duffle bags and wait for what seems like at least an hour but is probably only 15–20 minutes.

Heads are starting to dare to lift and look around and I find enough courage to join them. I start to get my bearings. *Okay, I'm on black asphalt and those are…surely not, I'm not even going to think it.* This is probably a holding area and we're going to march or something to our actual barracks where we'll be living for the next 5 months. Nope, the things I saw sitting on top of that black asphalt were in fact rows and rows of trailer homes. Trailer homes that were in fact going to be my home for the next 5 months. What did I expect, really? I just got off an actual livestock trailer on my way over here.

Looking out over the parking lot, my new front yard was a huge brand new complex complete with a running track and workout area. That complex was actually where 90% of Military Police recruits were being housed during their time in Ft. Leonardwood. We were the 10% that had to accept and thrive in the dirtbag role. We didn't need nice shit anyways… right? RIGHT?! *Crying face* Turns out those trailers were host to a bunch of wild shit and I'm thankful that I even made it through.

After we were done hurrying up to standing around, the yelling picked up again and we were given instructions by the first sergeant (a.k.a. the main guy in charge around here). The instructions seemed simple enough: get into formation, take off your belt with canteen on it, buckle it back up, place it on the ground in front of you with the buckle facing forward, then take your canteen out and place it to the right of your belt. Needless to say, we all did push-ups and got yelled at for the next 90 minutes because not EVERYONE could follow simple instructions.

After lots of moaning and groaning, some dorks started with the classic "come on guys we can do this" motivation. There were even some tears from those who had never been yelled at or done a push-up before. Eventually, we were back on our feet and done with that fun party. This is what is affectionately known as your first "smoke session" and we were promptly reminded by the first sergeant that the beatings would continue until morale improved. This basically meant that we were going to get yelled at and made to do push-ups until every last one of us did exactly what we were told to do when we were told to do it. Spoiler alert, that's impossible, so we got yelled at a lot and got super jacked over the next 5 months. Mass punishment is about as fun as going to the DMV to get your new license. Which, when you think about it is mass punishment in itself. So, same.

The rest of the afternoon was administrative stuff. We were assigned platoons based on what number line we got into coming off the cattle trailer (third platoon for me). We handed over our paperwork, so they knew who was who, then we were told who was who, what was what, where was where, and given the basic ground rules of the trailer park. Can't go into certain places, mainly the drill sergeant's office trailer and the female trailers. Then, we were given our trailer and bunk assignments; mine was at the back right corner of the trailer park with my bunk being by the back door next to the laundry room. Freedom was right outside that back door, the ultimate tease.

Each trailer held about 30 people and my bunkmate ended up being a 40-year-old named Crest. He happened to be the same guy that showed everyone how to put on a duffle back super-fast earlier in the day. We were the two oldest people there. He was 18 years older than me and had a wealth of Army knowledge from ROTC. We were told about fire guard: one hour per night where you sat at the desk in front of the trailer and counted everyone that was in there to make sure there were still 30 breathing bodies in there. If and when a drill sergeant came in to check those 30 bodies, you had to read a script from a piece of paper to report on those undead bodies in your care. Yes, drill sergeants had overnight shifts where they were literally babysitting sleeping children and making sure nobody was taken or ran away. Jeez. Surprisingly, nobody ever ran away from the trailer park. However, every so often someone would get caught sleeping while on fire guard duty and that's when the lights got turned on and we all "got to" do push-ups.

Looking back, it makes me believe it must be really fun to be a drill sergeant and have carte blanche on punishment when someone messes up at any point. Case in point, one night a guy named Ramirez had fireguard duty in my trailer and fell asleep. It wasn't the first time it had happened so everybody knew (or thought we knew) what we were in for when the lights came on and a loud voice carried all across the trailer. Being woken up by a screaming voice is something that you never get used to and have to work really hard on letting go of when you get out of the military. Anyways, that night Ramirez fell asleep and we were awoken by a screaming drill sergeant. Everyone hopped out of bed and started getting down into push-up position. But the drill sergeant who had busted Ramirez said, "No, no, no, privates, not yet. We have to tuck in little diaper baby Ramirez first." *Tuck him in? What's happening here? We don't have to do any push-ups? Is this a terrible dream? Should I just go back to sleep?*

Everyone is looking at everyone for 10 seconds or so before we hear the drill sergeant call everyone up to the front to gather around Ramirez. We had all become pretty numb to the yelling at this point so everyone was thinking what I was thinking: *Can't we just get yelled at, do some midnight push-ups, and go back to sleep?* Boy, oh boy were we in for a treat that was better than those push-ups. After we were done rubbing the sleep from our eyes and gathered around Ramirez; the drill sergeant announced that since Ramirez was soooo sleepy, we needed to tuck him into bed. He then proceeds to tell Ramirez to go lay down in his bed, close his eyes, and for all of us to form a single-file line facing his bed. Then, one by one, the drill sergeant told us to file by Ramirez's bed, pat his blanket around him, pat him on the head, and tell him goodnight and sweet dreams. So, we did just that. All 30 of us while trying not to bust out giggling like a pack of junior high volleyball players. When we had all gotten our turns tucking in Ramirez and whispering sweet nothings into his ear, we did end up having to do push-ups for the next 30 minutes. He was ordered to lay there and close his eyes while we finished. I'm pretty sure he actually fell asleep, but it was totally worth it for the lulz.

Another classic troll move by the drill sergeants was when a wall locker was found unlocked while we weren't in our trailers.

Each person had a wall locker and it had just the right amount of room for our uniforms, underwear, and maybe a drawer for our personal belongings. Our personal belongings only consisted of maybe a notebook and a Bible at best. Locking those wall lockers and TAKING THE KEY was a requirement and it was instilled in us that it was going to be like that the entire time we were in the Army. Honestly, I'm still not sure why. Was the enemy going to suddenly dash into this 5-star trailer and sniff my dirty tan underwear, steal my dirty boots and Kevlar helmet? Or maybe, just maybe, we should be worried about the dirtbags among our ranks that would steal our shit? Surely that couldn't be it, this is an honorable organization around here, right? RIGHT?! I digress.

When we would all leave for the day to go do whatever we had to do-ranges, obstacle course, classroom learning, ruck marches, and land nav, some drill sergeants would stay behind to do admin stuff. Admin stuff mostly meant that they sat around thinking of ways to troll us lowly ole privates, and probably just to take a break from babysitting us honestly.

As we talked about before, we always, always, always had to lock our stuff up when we left the trailer. No matter if you were just going outside to look at the sun, you better lock your shit up. Of course, we're always running behind schedule (so said the drill sergeants), so we were always rushed out the door. Our main goal was hoping that we had all the 150 items we needed jammed into various pockets both on our bodies and off. Sometimes, remembering to lock a wall locker was just not in the deck of cards that day. You would just plain 'ole forget or would make it look locked but not actually lock it all the way. This was easier because you didn't have to look for the key and then be responsible for the key while you're rolling around in the mud. Also, if you were in a hurry and needed something out of your wall locker you weren't having to fumble around with the lock. Number two was always a gamble. You were rolling the dice on whether a drill sergeant was going to actually give it a tug, keep walking on by, or not even check locks at all that day. Some days you could get away with it, but some days you would walk in from a long day of training, mud and sweat caked on you, smelling like swamp and ass, and somebody would have lost their lock gamble with the drill sergeant. Ahhhh, the smell of somebody fucked up. Can't forget that smell.

My personal favorite is one time after a short training day where we had the rest of the day off to do "bay maintenance". Bay maintenance is where you just kinda chill, do laundry, sweep, and mop then mop some more. It is a "always act like you're doing something" type of day. After training, we were buzzing on the walk into the trailer, knowing we were about to just chill. The lead man opened up the door and flipped on the lights. He immediately said, "OH SHIT", which caused all of us to run up the stairs to see what was going on. We stood on the threshold, almost in disbelief. The entire floor was covered in anything and everything that was tan or camo and I mean everything. Everyone's boots, undershirts, underwear, socks, uniform tops, bottoms, dress uniforms, blankets, sheets . . . all of it. The cherry on top of it all was that there were three very well-put-together scarecrow soldiers made of all the camo and tan parts of our uniforms with pillows as faces. Honestly, incredible craftsmanship. We were all just standing there staring at how well put together these scarecrow soldiers were.

Once we all took our jaws off the floor and slowly made our way inside, the real devastation set in. How were we going to sort through all of the underwear, shirts, uniforms, various military gear and get it back to its rightful owner? After we were all done standing around in disbelief, mouths agape, everyone started making their way to where their bunks and wall lockers *used* to be. We started what we knew would be a long and tedious process of going through a triple-wide that just got hit by a tornado.

As Private Perry, a good ole boy from Alabama whose bunk was dead center of our trailer, stepped out from the edges towards his former "bedroom"; a huge zombie-like body popped up from under the layer of camo and tan. It was just like the Undertaker during a buried alive match at WrestleMania. Bah gawd it's the Undertaker!!! There were a few audible shrieks and gasps and I'm pretty sure someone fainted coming out of the bathroom. We were all frozen in shock while trying to hold in both tears and laughter. The Undertaker, I mean drill sergeant, stood up and told us to go ahead and get down in the front leaning rest position (the top of the push-up). Man, I'm not even mad at you Drill Sergeant Undertaker, that was a good one. I'll gladly do some push-ups to entertain you.

As I was doing those well-deserved push-ups and the Drill Sergeant Undertaker was giving us the whole "ThIs Is WhY yOu DoNt LeAvE yOuR wAlL lOcKeR UnLoCkEd" speech, I glanced up at him and saw him smirking out the side of his mouth. I know he went back and told all his little drill sergeant friends how good he got us while they all laughed and high-fived and stuff. An eagle probably even squawked overhead. America. Fuck yeah.

Another time that sticks out to me was when a drill sergeant was being an absolute troll at a range. We were all waiting around after a range for our cattle trailer to arrive and whisk us back home to the trailer park. For the few days leading up to any range, the drill sergeants would actually be nice and respectful to us. We would watch *Black Hawk Down* to get us all riled up and in the big HOOOAH mood. They would even give us a good dinner and we were even "given" plenty of sleep the night prior. Turns out the performances of us little stinky privates at key events like shooting ranges were actually key performance indicators of how good a drill sergeant was at their job. We were basically being bribed with food, sleep, and entertainment to make all the drill sergeants look good on their performance evaluations and resumes. Sounds like an emotionally and physically abusive relationship to me, but what do I know, I'm just a stinky little private that can shoot lights out. After the ranges where we did well at and passed for our overlords, everyone was in a jovial mood. We were able to loosen up a bit, even if it was for 30 minutes.

On this particular day, it was one of our final ranges of the many we had over 5 months. As the sun was setting over the very pretty rolling hills surrounding Ft. Leonardwood there were about 100 of us sitting in these tall bleachers, quietly talking (wouldn't want us to get too rowdy, ya know). Then THE notoriously mean female drill sergeant comes strolling down front on ground level and we all shut the fuck up real quick. She yells back, "you all can keep talking, just keep it down". She then followed it with an astounding, "you did a great job today. I wouldn't say I'm proud of you guys, but today is an alright day, so whatever." This was a level of sharing we had never experienced from her over the course of the past 4 months or so. We were all so taken back by her calmness that it took us a quick minute to actually resume what we were doing. After 5 minutes or so of us bullshitting around, we heard her voice again and all expected it to be her yelling at us that we were done talking. That's alright, we got a solid amount of time in, so go ahead and yell at us to stop. We get it. Boy, oh boy, were we wrong. This notoriously mean, sadistic drill sergeant started going into a stand-up comedy routine!

Before we get into what her comedy routine was like and my ranking of it, we must pause so I can hopefully get you to grasp how much of a 180-degree turn this was for this particular drill sergeant. Every platoon within my basic training unit was assigned two to four drill sergeants specifically for that platoon, like a homeroom teacher in a sense. Every teacher (drill sergeant) in school (basic training unit) could tell you what to do and you could technically ask them questions if they were around, and you absolutely needed an answer. They know what's going on in a broad sense, but they don't know you or your platoon mates on a micro level. However, your homeroom teachers (platoon drill sergeant) really know you the best and you went to them first for any issue or question you had. You were with them the most, so you really got to know them. Well, as much as you could get to know a drill sergeant in basic training.

So, this particularly devilish homeroom drill sergeant was assigned to the second platoon. One day, about a week prior to the comedy routine incident, it was mid-June in Missouri and closing in on 100 degrees. A tale worthy of repeating was starting to come from the trailers that the second platoon inhabits. Tales like this one traveled quickly through our whole company by what's called the PNN–Private News Network. PNN's main source of "news" was all of us: the privates. Mostly rumors but some factual storytelling being passed from one group to another. Just like in modern-day news reporting, you always had to distinguish if what you were hearing had any foundation of truth and the source from which you were getting the information. In other words, the PNN was a big rumor mill but there was still valuable intel to be gained.

The PNN headline that was spreading like wildfire among the trailers had the aforementioned mean female drill sergeant as its main subject: "DRILL SERGEANT SUENO TURNED OFF THE AIR CONDITIONING AND FANS THEN SMOKED EVERYONE IN CHARLIE BAY FOR TWO HOURS STRAIGHT—NO WATER BREAKS." The subsequent story read like something out of a WW2 history book:

Sueno was so mad about the lack of cleanliness in her "homeroom" class in Charlie Bay. Instead of her usual yelling for such transgressions, Sueno decided to turn into the actual devil for the day. She turned poor Charlie Bay into her own fiery lake of fire and brimstone. With a twisted, evil grin on her face, Sueno instructs the nearest shivering private to go turn off the lights and close all the doors. The temperature in the room was already reading 95 degrees with 80% humidity outside. Sueno then calmly walked over to the locked thermostat box, opened it, and with a loud *click* that could be heard through the bay, turned OFF the air conditioning that was already having a hard time offering respite from the harsh conditions outside. With all the privates of Charlie

Bay standing there shell-shocked, that's when the punishment really began. They were taken through push-ups, sit-ups, cherry pickers, plank holds, and other various physical activities meant to punish and sweat. The collective body temperatures rose and sweat could be seen dripping from the mirrors in the bathroom. Charlie bay residents endured another 90 minutes of physical and mental torture. Sweat continued to pool up on the ground and silence filled the room as they all seemingly pushed a hole into the Earth's crust itself. By the 2-hour mark, a few lucky souls had passed out from heat exhaustion. That's when Sueno calmly walked back over to the locked thermostat box and clicked the switch back over to air conditioning "on", leaving Charlie Bay looking like a sauna warzone. Sweat and tears lay waste to everyone and everything in the bay. The walls were weeping with sweat, it was reported.

Jeez, was this PNN story actually true? It sounded completely horrid. The Charlie Bay people swore it was so and they had the scars on their soul to prove it. That PNN news story sums up everyone's thoughts and fears of drill sergeant Sueno and is the anchor as to why we were all so surprised sitting in those bleachers that night. Us in the bleachers were now her crowd to entertain as she started pacing her stage and doing "crowd work."

"Did you put on makeup today private?" she asked, pointing out a female in the third row.

"Ummmm, no drill sergeant I don't even have makeup here with me, and remember we aren't allowed."

"Damn, so you just look like a fucking clown naturally."

Oh. My. Goodness. Did we really just hear that? From who we thought we heard that from? Is this an alternate reality? Where am I? How did we go from devil reincarnated to Jerry Seinfeld so quickly? Don't worry, Sueno was just getting warmed up.

"Is your dad also your uncle and grandpa?" she asked, pointing at Pvt. Harris from Kentucky. My palms are sweaty, knees weak, you know the rest... As she continues her comedic rampage, all of us in the bleachers, otherwise known as the peanut gallery, start to get more and more animated in our responses. After an imitation of a completely illegal love affair going on between two privates (allegedly consummated in porta-potties on a range while nobody was watching) all of us in the peanut gallery couldn't hold it in any longer. We lost our minds and started hootin', hollerin', falling over each other, and yelling out, "OH SHIT." It was like we were free from prison, er, basic training being controlled by other adults. The peanut gallery was out of control and Sueno had to let us laugh ourselves out before going on with her stand-up comedy routine. After we had all calmed down enough to actually listen, she started pacing back and forth again with a smirk on her face. That's when she and I locked eyes and my smile quickly faded. It was like looking into the eyes of a bear—was it going to tear your face off or offer you honey like Winnie the Pooh? My brain was in a blender and I didn't know what to do. Turns out that 3 seconds of our eyes being locked was actually just her locking in her prey and getting ready to pull the trigger. Her bullet this time was a joke special just for me.

"Why the long face, Shotwell?!"

The peanut gallery was out of control with people now running around on the ground all around, screaming. So, I do have a long face with a pronounced chin and jaw under my current beard. She hit the nail right on the head and I could do nothing but laugh with all the peanuts laughing at me and nod my head. She got me. It wasn't necessarily the long-face joke that was the best one and that's why the peanut gallery went nuts. No, no, it was the anticipation of the next joke coming, mine just happened to be the culmination of all the previous jokes—a cherry on top.

It took everyone a couple of minutes to calm down and get back to even somewhat of a baseline. The peanut gallery was filled with hurting jaws from laughing so hard and tears rolling down their faces. After everyone was quiet again, she ended her tight 15 by telling us we all stink and wishes we wouldn't be in her Army. Perfect. A standing ovation and she disappeared to the side stage. A PNN report the next day said she made Charlie Bay do push-ups in the middle of the night "just cause." She was back in her natural form, but we got a glimpse of her alter ego, or maybe her actual self. We will never know. The world was back to its natural state. Perfectly balanced.

CHAPTER 4: SUGAR KING

"I'll trade you my whole tuna MRE for your Oreos."

–One of my Sugar Babies

The Silk Road was an ancient trade route that linked China all throughout Asia and Europe. It carried goods and ideas along a dangerous 4,000-mile stretch, spanning different countries and landscapes. Few people traveled the entire route alone; middlemen carried the goods and ideas between the two great civilizations of Rome and China. China received wool, silver, gold, and religious ideologies while Rome received silk and other fine tapestries. Illicit goods were also a large part of the Silk Road trade. The Silk Road proves that no matter what time of history you're talking about, there is someone somewhere that wants something they aren't supposed to have.

The military has an equivalent to the Silk Road, and I like to call it the Camo Road. Honestly, the similarities are astounding. Both include a large network of people that can acquire anything and everything you could ever want, no matter where you are. The Camo Road in basic training was the result of the melting pot that was all different people, cultures, ethnicities, and geographical locations before coming to the middle of nowhere Missouri to live in trailers in a parking lot (Ft. Leonardwood). We had people from Boston, Texas, California, Alabama, the Bronx, Manhattan, Queens, and Florida. Ethnicities of black, white, brown, and everything in between. Half a dozen languages were spoken in those trailers with the same number of dialects of the standard English language. Just like a prison. And what happens in prison? No, not that you sicko. Cliques form, things get smuggled in and those things get bought and sold (or kept for themselves to be enjoyed). Things can be "acquired" in prison and the person receiving said thing(s) doesn't want to know where it came from. Where there are people, there are people that want something they can't have. And we had a group of people living in a trailer park on hot asphalt that wanted stuff. The Camo Road always obliges…often at a steep price.

As soon as you get to basic training, your entire schedule and norms are no longer up to you. There are everyday comforts that used to be a part of everyday life that you will no longer have access to. There are major comforts that get restricted. These are typically the hardest to overcome and are always craved by all the stinky privates going through basic training: caffeine, sugar, tobacco, and communication with the outside world with a bonus being basic medical care. Imagine having to go through terrible coffee withdrawal headaches around a bunch of strangers, all the while getting yelled at by another more powerful stranger that can make you do anything they please. The same goes for tobacco and again the same for not being able to call bae back home. Maybe somewhat surprisingly, the toughest withdrawal for people to get over during my time at basic training was sugar. Everyone craved it. Everyone talked about their favorites. Everyone daydreamed about what their first sugar-filled treat was going to be as soon as they graduated. We couldn't have any of it. Not even one Skittle.

Don't even fucking look at it. For the first couple of months, sugar wasn't even available for us even on the good days. If we were eating MREs (meals ready to eat) and there were M&Ms or Skittles in there, you had to walk it over to your drill sergeant and give it to them, tears in your eyes. If there was ever a time when you wanted to make a mad dash for it and escape, it was when you were making that walk. Skittles in hand.

After about 2 months into basic training, we were allowed to start having sugar if it came in our MREs or if it was provided to us when we had Hot As brought to us. Hot A's is actual hot food brought out to a training site, think catering. It was a rarity but a huge hit when it did happen. Once the sugar ban was lifted... I became The Godfather of Sugar. The Camo Road authority on sugar. You came to me if you had a craving that needed to be fulfilled. You came to The Godfather humbly and ready to pay whatever I said to get that pack of Oreos, M&Ms or even a whiff of a Skittle. Remember, all the goods you're able to get via the Camo Road comes with a price. My price was usually your entire meal. Let me give you an example.

Say we're on a ruck march training mission where we ruck march six miles then do some weapons training at a range. We typically all sit and have a nice MRE lunch once we get to that range. Don't worry, you were never allowed to pick your MRE. They were thrown to us by drill sergeants instead You get what you got, deal with it. MREs typically come with a main "dish," a couple of sides, and a dessert (a.k.a. sugar). There's a hierarchy to MREs, with chili mac being at the top. Fight me. Everybody wanted the chili mac, but sometimes you got the pork patty. Sometimes that bottom of the barrel pork patty came with some good sides and a full-sized peanut M&M. After the drill sergeant passed out the MREs, they left to go eat their actual food lunch, leaving us stinky privates to our own devices.

This particular time was our first time eating unsupervised and meant that we could actually talk as long as we didn't get too crazy. What that also meant was that the Camo Road was immediately open for business. It was like the New York Stock Exchange floor on that rocky and muddy range site. Unwanted side dishes were being held up for trade. There were trade offers, trade denials, and even tears at having to eat a cold pork patty AGAIN. I opened my MRE, realized there was a full-sized peanut M&M in there, closed it up, and slowly started eating the tuna and crackers that came in there. Once everyone had made their trades and sat back down, I calmly stood up, cleared my throat, and announced that I had a full-sized peanut M&M that I didn't want. The ant pile had been stepped on.

"I'll give you my crackers and cheese."

"Take my power bar."

"Mashed potatoes."

"Apple sauce."

I could see the desperation in their eyes and felt like a king that was handing out bread to peasants. All of those were pretty good offers and I definitely would have taken most of them. Until the market got set and a young handsome Bostonian in the back stood up in the back and in his thick, powerful Boston accent said,

"I'll give you my whole chili mac for those M&Ms." Be sure to read that last line in a Boston accent as best you can. It makes it more dramatic. Hearing those words gave me a rush of power that can only be equated to Vito Corleone in the opening scene of The Godfather.

There were gasps of envy and shock that rippled through that small crowd. Everyone knew that was my coronation and I was now the King of Sugar when I took that trade. They could come to me with a respectful offer and I would take care of their sugar sickness with whatever sugar I had. They'd give up their day's nutrition for a hit of sugar...and like it. Kiss the sugar ring or be sick, you pick.

I now had constituents of sugar babies at my disposal. I ate like an actual king that day at lunch with a grin on my face. To me, I had just pulled a fast one over on the Bostonian. I looked over at him, though, and he was grinning as big as I was. He was letting those peanut M&Ms melt in his mouth while he was lying on his back looking at the sky. Like a crackhead.

The MRE Sugar King is one thing, but my power was taken to a whole different universe on the days we got Hot A's. I stuffed my long face with a buffet of eggs, chicken on the bone, and Gatorade. When the Hot As arrived, I was holding court. Every time. Guaranteed.

Breakfast hot As in the middle of nowhere Missouri come with various single-serve cereals: Froot Loops, Frosted Mini-Wheats, Lucky Charms, Cheerios, and a whole milk carton. That's as far as my sugar babies saw or cared about. They wanted a double portion of those Lucky Charms and they were going to give their Sugar King their scrambled eggs, bacon, and potatoes to get it. I would have the equivalent of three Denny's Grand Slams while the sugar babies were eating 300 calories of cereal. I couldn't believe it…while I was stuffing my face with crispy bacon. If you want to see the face of addiction, look no further. Hot A's lunch would be the same but substitute the eggs and bacon with a quarter rotisserie chicken and baked potato. All for a little baby sleeve of Oreos. Sugar babies need their sugar. The Sugar King is a firm but fair king. By the time dinner rolled around and they were starving but still needing their hit of sugar, I wouldn't take their main course, the nutritious part of their dinner. No, no, no, my little sugar babies needed their energy. So, I would let them keep the chicken, rice, and cookies; then give them my cookies with an IOU of $10 from them. By the end of basic training, I had the easiest $300 I ever earned.

The Sugar King was really only the Sugar King when we were out in the field, away from the trailers. The reason was, once we were a couple of months into basic training we were allowed to start getting "care packages" from home 'This meant it was an absolute free for all. So much so that our overlords, er, drill sergeants would have us believe that mail just didn't come very often during that time. They would lie to us, just like a parent lying to their kid about the Easter Bunny, by saying the classic "mail must have gotten lost this week privates." Oh really, the United States Postal Service, which is trusted to deliver bills, checks, voting results, junk mail, and fucking Anthrax in the '90s is all of a sudden losing all of our packages at the same time? ORRRR could it be that you guys just don't want to deal with the sugar babies and fanatical riots that come from potentially getting a package of Skittles and some ChapStick from home? Can't say that I blame them. It was pandemonium when the mail came. Always. The biggest and only important thing that care packages could include? You guessed it… Sugar. You didn't have to settle for whatever the MRE or hot As gave you. You could get your favorite candy shipped right to your trailer park in the middle of Missouri. Fuck those letters from home and how everyone was doing—WE WANT THE SUGAR. WE WANT THE SUGAR!!

Beyond the packages not actually showing up with any regularity, there was one caveat that brought everyone down to earth…You only had 5 minutes or sometimes less to eat whatever you could out of your package. This included the items from multiple packages from weeks prior that have now backed up and all arrived at the same time. They did get lost (not ever picked up from the post office) remember? Five minutes to put as much diabetes as you can into your suck hole. Five minutes to glory my little babies. That first time those care packages showed up instantly boosted morale by 420%. Skittles were being swallowed whole, Reese's Cups stacked on top of each other, Snickers were being treated like an eggplant (you get it), RIP the Sour Patch Kids that were being murdered by the dozen. Sugar babies with no restraint. The black asphalt looked like a movie theater dumpster tipped over. At the end of the 5 minutes, mouths still full of M&Ms, everyone looking like Joey Chestnut after the July 4th hotdog eating contest. We had to do push-ups for every bit of trash that was left on the ground. Spoiler alert, it was a lot. We got to see what a lot of our favorite candy looks like coming back up.

This is where the Camo Road was born. Out of that harrowing experience. We were stuffing candy anywhere we could: mouths, underwear, socks, and wherever else candy packaging could fit. This candy had a different destination: the Camo Road. Back to the trailers to be hidden among blankets, socks, behind washing machines, anywhere and everywhere. That candy had trade value. Those who could smuggle well and weren't afraid to stick a pack of Skittles in their taint would wield an intoxicating power. Some would go on to get busted and be given extra work or extra push-ups, but others would go on to have successful Camo Road careers. Careers of shuttling candy from one trailer to the other. One person to the next person. Sugar baby to sugar baby.

At the end of the day, my sugar babies and I were an integral part of the Camo Road, each of us receiving what we needed and wanted. You see, I always wanted to eat as much protein and nutrition as I could because I honestly didn't know when we would be eating again sometimes. I was aware of properly fueling my body before I came to basic training and was aware of fueling my body the best I could once I got to basic training. Choosing as much protein and fresh fruit as I could, whenever I could, was going to give my body the best chance to have enough energy to make it through. I had too much willpower and didn't even think about eating the desert when it became available. Why would I? I had decided I couldn't have it, so I'm not going to have it. That was my mentality. Protein > sugar. Real high-level meathead stuff, that's why I awarded myself a doctorate in "Broscience."

Sugar babies let their cravings and emotions run free and convinced themselves they NEEDED the sugar, which maybe they did. Everyone made it through basic training, so who am I to deprive them of their own personal needs?

CHAPTER 5: SICK CALL

"Sure, go to sick call if you're a wuss."

–A sergeant somewhere

Basic medical needs in the military, especially during basic training, are not like what we have out in the "civilian world". We weren't even allowed to have basic over-the-counter medicine like Dayquil, allergy medicine, or even Tylenol during basic training. You had to essentially get prescribed such basic medicines by another adult. Ones that you're used to walking right into a CVS and grabbing off the shelf yourself. There are also psychological aspects to being sick or hurt in the military, especially during basic training. Everyone from the drill sergeant down to your bunkmate (fuck, even from yourself) was questioning your motives.

"Am I going to get told by a doctor that I can't do certain things? Would I have to be in this fucking trailer park for even longer than I expected?" being chief among those questions. Aside from your own personal fears of having to live in the said trailer park for even an hour past your scheduled time of leaving, there is an overall skepticism among drill sergeants and your peers about your "sickness". The military always has different names for things than the outside world. In this case, we call urgent care *sick call.*

Sick call is where you go if you're sick, if you twisted your ankle, or think you pulled a muscle. Typical stuff that you would go see your general practitioner down the road for. Instead of just hopping in your car or catching the bus to your doctor back home; you have to ask permission from another adult to go see a doctor in the military. A call to arms for the sickly ones. Almost 100% of the time you end up being able to go to sick call, but it's not without passive-aggressive comments from everyone around you. There's even a name for someone who is always sick and going to sick call: Sick Call Ranger or Profile Rider. There's an assumption that you don't want to do the hard stuff and that you're somehow letting the "team" down by going and taking care of yourself. Imagine every time you get sick and end up going to see the doctor you get chastised for it. Ridiculed by everyone in your house and on your block. Looked down on and told you are lazy and weak for seeking out medical treatment. Sounds like shit, doesn't it? That's how it is when you ask to go to sick call in the military though. That's not to say that there are people that do go to sick call just because they don't feel like doing anything that day and want to get out of it. I've seen it with my own eyes. It happens, but it's the minority.

The drill sergeants would use the fact that nobody wanted to stay any extra days and be held back from graduating basic to stop people from going to sick call. It was psychological warfare, and they were good at it. There was a time during the winter months during my trailer park stay when the flu absolutely ravaged a bunch of us. High fevers, coughing, body aches, and other obvious flu stuff. Nobody wanted to miss out on "very important training that could hold you back if you miss it," so most of us just pushed through those couple of days. That psychological warfare around sickness really did toughen all of us up and show us that you can do stuff while you're sick. I also let it swing me too far to that side and it took me years to allow myself to rest when I got sick.

There are some at-home remedies to certain ailments that I learned during this time. Being persuaded not to go to sick call in basic training made you get creative. I still use a lot of those remedies even 10 years afterward. Like this one. Did you know that pouring bleach on poison ivy or poison oak is a great natural at-home remedy?! Yeah, yeah it actually makes it stop itching and dries it up in no time! It also burns all the other skin around it, making new blisters, cracks, and overall uncomfortableness. I found this out the hard way during the land navigation part of basic training.

Our land navigation course is in the woods of the Ozarks; a whole day of getting lost up, down, left, and right in the middle of those woods. Those woods that are filled with poison ivy and poison oak. You don't really have a choice in looking out for them since you're barely confident in the direction you're headed in the first place. You're too focused on that compass, azimuth, and map to even care if you're walking right through a big patch of poison ivy. So yeah, a lot of us came back with nice red, itchy rashes to show how lost we actually got. Do you think we all came back and went straight to get at the very least Calamine lotion? Yeah, not a fucking chance. Of course not. We got fed the old line of what if the nurse at sick call told us that we couldn't do training tomorrow and we had to get held back? But don't you worry, on the bright side, we got some good old-fashioned military Broscience taught to us by a drill sergeant. You guessed it: "Just put some bleach on it, it will dry out the oily poison ivy in no time, and you'll be able to keep training! No big deal privates, it doesn't even look like it itches."

So instead of going to get some actual medicine, we all decided to give it a try. We went inside our trailers and began folding up paper towels. We then poured some off-brand bleach on the paper towels before scrubbing down the festering poison oak blisters and poison rashes. Yeah, it burned. Yeah, the smell of bleach and burning flesh was awful. Yeah, it was just a horrible idea overall! Necks, hands, feet, arms, and ankles were all getting chemical burns by those bleach-soaked paper towels. But I tell you what, the next morning, nobody was itchy and the festering rashes had cleared themselves right up. Probably not the most medically sound advice I'll ever receive but it will do in a pinch if you're stranded in a cabin in the middle of the woods and there happens to be a bottle of bleach under the kitchen sink...feel free to use it.

Another quick one for you guys: Did you know that cough drops basically cure everything? Yeah, actually studies by every drill sergeant ever have shown that strep throat, sore throat, the flu, the common cold, headaches, lack of energy, and upper respiratory infections can all be cured by a simple off-brand cough drop. I know what you're thinking: *Whoa, there's no way that could be right. Where are the peer-reviewed studies to show that?* Don't ask such silly questions, that's just the way it is. Cough drops actually became a major part of the Camo Road and ironically provided by the people that went to sick call, a.k.a. the doctor the most. The Sick Call Rangers and profile riders were looked down upon by everyone, but they had found their place among the masses. Getting "prescribed" cough drops then selling them or giving them out to beggars. Cough drops quickly became high in demand and with good reason…they cure everything. So next time you feel yourself having the flu or strep throat, don't go to the doctor. You might miss work, and nobody wants that. Just reach for a cough drop instead.

Paid for by big cough drop corporations

CHAPTER 6: DEODORANT GOAT

"What's in the boxxxxx?"

–Not Brad Pitt in *Seven*

This story could be a short film of its own. A story of international intrigue, lies, deception, secrecy, and romance. It has it all. Okay, maybe it's not that in-depth and maybe it doesn't have the international intrigue part either. Nonetheless, it's hilarious. It is the equivalent of *The Italian Job* but for basic training. One none of the drill sergeants had ever seen before. First, we need to meet the main character in the story: Bradley.

Bradley is a baby-faced kid from Alabama, who, by the time we got to the trailer park was already second-guessing his decision to give up his life to the military for the next 4 years. He didn't really give a shit about much. He was overall lazy, was a sugar baby, but above all else was hilarious to everyone. He had a deep southern accent and a little potbelly that somehow grew larger while we were in basic training. His overall disdain for the military already made us all laugh and he only needed to speak one word to get us rolling on the floor cracking up. Bradley was always talking about what he was gonna do when he got home.

"Shotwell, I got like five girls waitin' on me when I get back to Mobeeele (Mobile, AL). They think I'm a war hero already and I'm not going to correct them, man. We're going to go out to this fish fry, get fucked up, and all just fuck each other, man."

And he would say it to me basically every day. The thought of that fish fry and orgy really kept him going throughout the day and sometimes kept me going, too.

A fish fry and orgy does sound nice Bradley, you're right.

"Shiiiit man then come on down to Mobeele. I got you, dude."

Nah, I'm good Bradley. I wouldn't want to get in the way of family business.

That one went over his head and if it went over yours, go ask somebody. Anyways, is Bradley the southern Big Lebowski? Maybe. Probably. As you may have guessed by now, there's not a ton of communication with the outside world during basic training, especially the first few months. If you're lucky, you would get 5 minutes on a payphone once every 2 weeks to call wherever and let them know you're still alive and doing well. *Wink wink.* Absolutely no cell phones. Those got taken away at in-processing, remember? The whole no weapons, cell phones, and dildos speech? Yeah, that place just making sure you remembered. Your only outside communication was via a calling card (you paid for) on a pay phone or good ole fashioned pen to paper. It was weeks before your letter got to someone and received a letter back, so it was kinda pointless. Thanks, Army, you cheap fucks can't even make the payphones free huh? Whatever.

For many of the guys and gals, basic training is the first time in their lives they've been away from their family for more than a day. Much less 5 months. Similar to sugar, we become addicted to other humans and felt like we need to be connected with them every day. That's the reason why Bradley and almost everyone else talked about what they were going to do as soon as they got home. It was the best way to deal with the withdrawals. However, unlike sugar, there's absolutely nothing anybody could do about their communication withdrawals. Or so we thought . . .

My bunk was situated inside the trailer on the very back wall next to the emergency exit door (see diagram below). Just to the right of my bunk, in the corner, was the laundry room with washers and dryers and a heavy steel door to keep out the noise and smell. Caddy corner to my bunk and on the opposite side of the laundry room was Bradley's bunk. To the right of Bradley's bunk were the bathroom and showers. I loved my bunk spot for a few reasons. First, drill sergeants always came through the front door, so I had ample opportunity to get up and not get caught doing something I wasn't supposed to be doing. Second, I could sit back and people-watch: observe what everyone was doing and take it all in. Lastly, every single person in my trailer had to walk by my bunk to get into the laundry room. There was no getting past it. I was going to see your face, say what's up (or not), joke around with you, and smell all your smelly socks.

There were technically only certain hours that you could do your laundry, with us having a bedtime and all. We would all break that rule from time to time and do our laundry past bedtime if we needed to. There were only four washers and four dryers that worked for the 30 of us so there was typically a line. I always wake up at least once in the middle of the night to go pee, and that didn't stop during basic training. But one night, about 2 weeks after moving into the trailers, as I was getting myself cozy again on a bed that was too short for me, I heard what sounded like whispering coming from what I thought was the laundry room. *There's no way,* I think to myself. *Nobody would dare even be out of their beds roaming around, much less talking to someone else.*

A drill sergeant might actually murder one of us if we were out of our beds being a chatty Cathy with another stinky private in the middle of the night. That night, I just chalked it up to me being tired and sleepy and fell right back to sleep. I didn't think anything of it and had convinced myself I was actually hearing things. The next 3 months went by and after so long of hearing things, those voices in the laundry room became a subconscious white noise. It had become a habit; I get up to pee and noise is coming from the laundry room. *That's just the way this world works.* I thought, until the 3-month mark when the truth of the laundry room voices came to light.

Diagram 1: My Trailer

Three months into basic training and two to go, and we still only had access to payphones and mail. Both were more frequent than at the start, but still not an everyday occurrence. So everyone was still talking about what they were going to do when they got home as a way of coping. The end of basic is near so Bradley has really begun to ramp up his fish fry and orgy excitement. He even adds a new girl or two to the event. I'm still hearing voices coming from the laundry room but that might as well be the Ghost of Christmas Past in there talking to Santa Claus himself.

Every few weeks, drill sergeants would come to inspect our trailer, personal wall lockers, beds, and our overall cleanliness. We'd usually be given an afternoon on a weekend to get everything cleaned with a toothbrush and organized. It was also a heads-up to get rid of anything you're not supposed to have. At the end of that cleanup afternoon, there would be all kinds of shit in the trash can: Snickers, gummy bears, condoms (wtf are y'all even doing?). No dildos that I saw, but it had the same vibe as that first night of in-processing; repentance of our sins. The next morning after breakfast, it was our trailer's time to get everything inspected. There would be lots of hurrying up and waiting. A strength of ours by this point. There was always some yelling, some push-ups, and then we would be on our way. That's how it normally went at least. This day would change the course of how inspections were done in basic training for generations to come. All thanks to Bradley.

If you remember, Bradley's bunk was around the corner from mine in the back. This gave us a solid 45-minute wait of just standing next to our bed while the drill sergeant made his way around the trailer. *Clean this, move that, hangers go here, boots go here instead of there, your bed looks like shit, do 20 push-ups.* That was the routine for the drill sergeant, or close to it. Of course, I look over and Bradley is lying down on his bed. An example of him not giving one single fuck. I giggle to myself like always because really I'm in total admiration of not being able to give a shit about anything. Drill sergeant makes his way around to my bunk, it's fine. He yells at me to do some push-ups just for existing, then he's on to Bradley's bunk.

Bradley's inspection starts off pretty typical. The drill sergeant looks around, swipes his hand for dust on top of the locker, moves some stuff around to look for dildos, jingles the pants, opens the toiletries bag, dumps it out (gotta make sure there's not any crack cocaine in there). Then it got weird. When the toiletries bag got dumped and the drill sergeant was moving stuff around, he froze. The drill sergeants never freeze. They always keep it moving because they don't want to be in that trailer any more than we do. But this time, his head turned as if he was a wolf listening for a moose in the woods. What did he hear?! Then he starts picking things up out of the toiletries bag and dropping them again, trying to replicate where that noise came from. You know like when you're home alone as a kid and there's a random noise so you go around kicking stuff trying to get it to make that same noise so you won't be so scared anymore. Same way. Nail clippers weren't it, the toothbrush wasn't it, soap holder wasn't it, Q-Tips package wasn't it. My heart is racing at this point. It's so out of the ordinary for a drill sergeant to be doing all this just for some noise that he specifically heard and I completely missed. It was like I was living and breathing a true crime documentary on ABC's 20/20. A glance over at Bradley and he wasn't even the slightest bit red, not worried about anything at all. Maybe it's all nothing and the drill sergeant is just being silly and trolling Bradley. Trying to get him to think something is big-time wrong. Then one of the two Old Spice sticks gets picked up. You know the ones: red container with the green stripe and blue gel deodorant once you open the cap. You can smell it right now and if you can't just imagine what a college dude in a dorm room smells like, that's what Old Spice Pure Sport smells like. It's also probably the official smell of the United States Army. Well, that and Marlboro Lights.

Anyways. The drill sergeant picks up one of *those* Old Spice Pure Sport sticks and begins to stare at it. He turns it over, drops it, picks it back up again, shakes it, drops it again. He looks at us lookin' at him, then picks it up again and finally opens it. Why were there two deodorants in the toiletry bag? A little odd, I think to myself but again, no cause for concern.

I see the slightest tinge of pink starting to form in Bradley's cheeks. What is happening!? I get on my tiptoes to see if I can see anything over him from my position. Okay, whew! There's that glorious blue gel under the cap, so there's nothing in there. But why is the drill sergeant still looking at it so intently then? Omg, why is he now twisting the cap getting the blue to go up and down? Now everyone is staring, involving themselves in this true crime doc that is unfolding right before our own eyes. It's twisting just fine so it must be just a typical stick of Old Spice, right? Nothing to see here. Until...he shakes it again. He shakes it really hard this time, with the blue twisted really far out. The blue part pops out and hits the ground. It was so quiet in that trailer that it sounded like someone had eaten Taco Bell right before church and then let out a loud Taco Bell fart during communion. That loud.

Bradley's face is suddenly bright red and pale all at the same time. He was the ghost of the Kool-Aid Man and we all still needed answers. The drill sergeant slowly turned his head toward Bradley who was doing anything to not make eye contact. After what seemed like 2 hours, but was probably only 2 minutes, the two make eye contact and time is frozen. An entire trailer full of people are now holding their breaths in anticipation. We needed to know what was happening at the bunk between the laundry room and bathroom. The main question in front of us now is what is with the Old Spice container that has caused this. WHAT COULD IT BE?! WHAT'S IN THE BOXXXXXX?

The drill sergeant methodically turns his head towards Bradley who is now standing stiff as a board at the position of attention, eyes forward, transfixed on a different dimension. He hadn't stood so still the entire 3 months we had been there so far. But now? Now he's paying complete attention. The drill sergeant, still holding the Old Spice Pure Sport without the blue part, tells Bradley to hold out his hand. So he does. The drill sergeant puts the bright red Old Spice stick in his hand and waits. He waits, and waits, and waits for what feels like 30 minutes but was probably 90 seconds in all.

We were all standing there, eyes affixed on the fish fry and orgy king from Alabama, waiting with bated breath. Then, in a super calming, fatherlike voice, the drill sergeant asked, "What's in there?" It was a simple question and one that at this point we all wanted to be answered. What *IS* in there Bradley?! I'm sure everyone had their suspicions and had become detectives while we waited but there's no way any of us was right.

Bradley, with the classic criminal line when the cops find cocaine in their purse "I don't know drill sergeant, I've never seen that there before." Everyone in the trailer collectively lets out an "aww, tiiisk." We already know. Bradley is fucked. We don't know for what, but the drill sergeant has him on something dead to rights. Bradley no longer looks like the ghost of the Kool-Aid Man. He's the color of the Kool-Aid Man himself, the reddest red you've ever seen. Drill Sergeant darts his eyes around towards all of us with the slightest smirk, in an acknowledging type of way. As if to say, "yeah, you guys know he's fucked huh?"

He tells Bradley to turn the deodorant upside down and give it a good shake into the drill sergeant's hand. This is it. The moment of truth where we find out who the killer is during this episode of 20/20 we're living through right now. Bradley closes his eyes, says his last prayer, and turns the deodorant over, giving it a couple of good shakes in the process. And…find out next week on Jerry Springer what was in the deodorant…

Just kidding, no cliffhangers here. He shakes it and out pops a Ziploc bag with a…with a…Is that a? Thirty sets of squinty eyes are now locked into that one hand with a Ziploc bag. It has a black something or another and what looks like a rope. No way that could be what we're thinking it is. The drill sergeant opens up the Ziploc bag and pulls out the black box thing. It's small, shiny, and about 3 by 2 inches if I had to guess. A flip phone! A Nokia flip phone!

Next, he holds it up over his head in triumph. Like he is at a fishing tournament and the winning bass is getting held up for all to see, near and far. But this time the winning bass at the national fishing tournament is a small black flip phone. Jaws are on the floor, heads are shaking, some in admiration, some in jealousy. Jealous of how the Alabama fish orgy guy who didn't give a shit about anything was able to have a cell phone this whole time while we all had to worry about if our calling card had enough minutes on it to call back home. I was impressed This was *Italian Job*-level at hiding something; *Oceans Twelve*-level sophistication. Bradley had really somehow found a way to hide a small flip phone in the bottom of a deodorant. Incredible.

After parading around all of us with his bounty held high, making sure we all had a chance to see the magical deodorant cell phone, the drill sergeant broke the silence in the room and said in a very eager voice, "EVERYONE SIT DOWN IN A CIRCLE, IIIIT'S STORY TIME WITH Bradley." We all gladly did. Bradley was too far gone for any of us to even remotely save him, so we wanted to have front-row seats to watch him burn like the degenerates we are. We were all sitting like giggling schoolgirls in our perfect circle, smiling from ear to ear. I looked over and the drill sergeant was taking his hat off and plopping down along the circle, just as excited as the rest of us to hear how we got here. Straight from Alabama George Clooney himself.

"Come right in the middle here and have a seat Bradley. We're all glad you're here and excited to hear from you" the drill sergeant says with a smirk on his face.

No doubt, we all have hundreds of push-ups, sit-ups, cherry-pickers, and flutter kicks to do after this, but for now everyone is relishing this entertainment opportunity.

"Now Bradley, remember, this is the circle of trust here. I'm just going to ask you some simple questions. Answer them as truthfully and completely as possible." The drill sergeant had suddenly lowered his tone and was compassionate and loving; he was now Drill Sergeant Oprah. Bradley nods and the interrogation begins.

"Let's start from the beginning Bradley, shall we? State your full name and where you're from."

"Tommy Bradley and I'm from Mobeeele Alabama."

"Good, good Bradley. You're doing great so far."

This prompted snickers from us in the trust circle. This was going better than expected.

"Bradley, why don't you explain to everyone here in this circle what exactly was in that Old Spice Pure Sport container. How did it get there? And why?"

Bradley then flipped a switch and understood the assignment. He was relishing in this circle of trust we had going on. He was Tom Cruise doing a tell-all on Oprah now. So, for the next 30 minutes, Bradley rips off his detailed planning and execution of the Old Spice cell phone heist. We were all mesmerized sitting around that circle, it was like an eyewitness account of Bigfoot. The son of a bitch had done it. He had pulled off having a cell phone in basic training. Here's how he did it, through the words of the now immortalized fish fry orgy King of Alabama himself: Tommy Bradley.

"It all started," Bradley says as he takes a big breath and looks around the circle at all of us, drill sergeant troll boy included. "When I started telling all my little honeys around town that I had joined the Army and was going to be leaving them to go off to basic training, boy, oh boy, were they sad. They couldn't believe I was going to be gone for 5 whole months and that I probably wouldn't be able to talk to them. The good news is they had all decided that I was already a bona fide hero by even going into the Army, so I got lots and lots of lovin' if you know what I mean." Our eyes all rolled at this one, *I'm sure dude.*

"As the days grew closer and closer to when I shipped off to basic, I started thinking of a way to be able to talk to them and make sure I had some lovin' to come back to when I got home to Mobeeele. They needed me" Bradley said.

He continued to explain that it had dawned on him one night on a beer run at the EZ Stop down the road. Half drunk and looking over the cigarette options, the light hits a bright green plastic package just right. "As if it was a sign from God," he exclaims!

"It was this little flip phone with 1,000 minutes already preloaded on it. I threw down a 100-dollar bill and didn't get no change back nor a pack of smokes, but I was on my way out of there with something I could work with. As soon as I woke up the next morning, I started packing for basic training. My recruiter sent me a list of stuff to bring so I laid it out all on my bed and started figuring out how I could hide this little cell phone. I had heard stories about all of your stuff being thrown around and searched as soon as we get here so I needed it to be good. My honeys were counting on their American Hero, and I wasn't going to let them down," he laughed. By the way, honeys is his word, not mine, thank goodness. We all laughed with him on this one because we all knew that he was far from it, he didn't give a shit is all.

"I was rifling through underwear, socks, paper, and pens. Then I honed in on my toiletry bag. That was it, I could figure out a way to put it in there! Could I sew a false pocket in there, I thought? No, too much trouble and you could have felt it from the outside anyways. I was just about to give up when I noticed the stick of deodorant. I picked it up and started moving it around, held up the flip phone to it and sure enough, I think it would fit! I just needed to actually get the phone in there somehow now. DID YOU GUYS KNOW YOU CAN TWIST THAT BLUE THING ALL THE WAY OUT THEN IT'S A HOLLOW COMPARTMENT UNDERNEATH?!" Bradley says with a burst of excitement."

"Yeah, we do now, dipshit," comes the response from drill sergeant troll boy still sitting cross-legged on the floor with us.

"Yeah, so sure enough, it fit right on in there, but I had to put it in a Ziploc so it wouldn't get all gooey and wouldn't rattle when you shook it. When I went to put the actual blue part deodorant thing back in, it wouldn't fit all the way down, so I had to cut off most of the blue stuff to get the lid back on. I knew we would eventually have a chance to buy our own toiletry stuff once we got here so I need to just hold off on using all of what was left until then. The honeys were excited when I told them I would be able to talk to them almost every day. I was basically Captain America in their eyes. The hard part was done, I just needed to pack up and head off to basic. I got through in-processing and the bag search with no problem, just the 500th Old Spice Pure Sport stick they had seen that day. After that, I just needed a few days to get a lay of the land and see what the middle of the night was like. Were there any drill sergeants lurking around and where were some good hiding spots would be to get on the phone. I found out real quick that laundry rooms were good because of the noise from the machines and the thick door that's meant to block out noise."

"It's been you talking on the phone in the laundry room this whole time?!" I blurted out. Bradley didn't even glance over at the drill sergeant at this point, he was too far gone. It wasn't going to matter what else he admitted to.

"Yep," he says, "the girls back home need to talk to me every day, man. I couldn't help it! It holds a pretty good charge, so I only needed to charge it about once a week. I would just stand in the bathroom in the middle of the night and let it charge there. If I heard a noise that sounded like a drill sergeant coming in during the night while it was charging or when I was talking on it, I would grab the charging cable and phone and stuff it in my shorts. Start rubbing my eyes and go just go back to bed" He was on a roll and was determined to finish up his tell-all to Oprah at this point.

"I would take it to ranges and any other training stuff we would do outside of the trailer park." He said. This one got the drill sergeant. He broke his Oprah character and blurted out in drill sergeant voice, "you did fucking what?!?!" Oopsies Bradley, you made the drill sergeant's face really red so maybe a bit too far. Nah, we've come this far. Finish him, Bradley. You could see Bradley thinking about it for about 2 seconds then he let it fly, "That's right drill sergeant. I would take it to ranges and stuff because I knew all of the drill sergeants would be out making sure we all didn't shoot ourselves or each other. Easy time to pop behind the bathroom or a tree and talk to one of the honeys."

Dear God, this man had no shame and we couldn't get enough. He was getting daily, sometimes hourly, updates from the outside world. Meanwhile, we were all living a *Little House on the Prairie* lifestyle. Waiting around and hoping a letter would come with news from back home as if we were in the trenches of WW1 or something. Bradley was living in 2150 while we were all stuck in the past. Now here we are, sitting in this circle with a drill sergeant and Bradley. Bradley just ended his speech with his signature shrug and half eye roll.

We were all looking around like *umm do we give him a standing ovation or is that too much?* Yes or no? Stand or no stand? Clap or no clap? We decided to just laugh and half-clap, maybe a whistle from the back. You gotta give it to the guy. That's a hell of a story, regardless of if you're in basic training or not. It's a testament to his relentlessness, resourcefulness, and fearlessness. No fear of repercussions, or maybe he just didn't think he would get caught. He had made it this far, so can you blame him for being a little arrogant?

So how much did the Old Spice flip phone cost ole Bradley? Extra duty for 15 days, forfeiture of pay for 15 days, 5,000 push-ups, and no phone privileges the rest of the 2 months we were there. Even when we all got to have our cell phones for 30 minutes or so, Bradley got nothing. The best part was that he had to make a 5-foot-tall cardboard cutout of an Old Spice deodorant stick (complete with the classic green stripe that designates the timeless Pure Sport scent) and then wear it around anytime we were cleaning up the trailer park or eating chow. It never got old and we would all crack up every time he put on that ridiculous piece of cardboard and pranced around.

The day Bradley sat in that trust circle is the day an official holiday at all basic trainings everywhere was made: Old Spice Smuggling Day. Yeah, you buy a nice new thing of Old Spice (must be Pure Sport) and hide something in it to see if your drill sergeant can find it. It's good training for them, so give it a shot and write back. I'm fairly certain that the way drill sergeants everywhere searched toiletry bags changed because of Bradley, and for that, he should keep his head high. I wonder if his fish fry orgy went the way that he had hoped?

Chapter 7: "Release Day"

"Don't ever try to contact me ever . . . for real don't."

—Your favorite drill sergeant the last time you see them

Graduation Day. Five long but also short months of living in a trailer park on a hot and iced-over asphalt parking lot. We shoveled snow with our hands, swept ice, painted rocks, cleaned toilets with toothbrushes, shot a bunch of guns, threw grenades, learned how to sleep anywhere, and bonded with people different from us. But now it was time to fly little birdies, fly!

With about 10 days until graduation, we were done with our training and all that was left was cleaning all of our gear. We didn't know we were really starting to learn a trait that would carry over into the rest of our time in the Army: pretending like you're busy and having other people do shit like cleaning a tent that has dirt all over it. Don't act like you're so righteous and don't know what I'm talking about. It's called shamming and everyone in the Army, and likely all the other branches know about it. As we've learned so far, the military isn't all guns and grenades all the time. In fact, it's not even *mostly* guns and grenades. I still had hope to be Captain America, after all, there were still two wars going on, right?

The overall vibe those ten days can only be described as elation and the biggest case of Senioritis you've ever seen. It's like when the inmates only have a week left before they're released from prison. They start getting chummy with the guards, thinking maybe they're friends. That was us with the drill sergeants. We thought we were invincible at that point. We were so close to getting out of there after all, what could they do to us anyways? Don't worry, a lot of push-ups were still done during those 10 days.

Also, about 2 weeks before our actual release date, er, graduation day, those of us on active duty got our duty station assignments (where we were going to be stationed). Boy, oh boy, did the big green weenie show me favor that day. Remember during in-processing when we got to pick our wish list for duty stations, but it's really about as powerful as your Christmas list to Santa? So, for S&Gs (shits and gigs), I put Germany, Italy, and Hawaii at the top of my list. No expectation of any of those ever happening. There I was, sitting in the trailer parking lot, sweating my ass off with a sunburn on my head. Hard not to have a sunburn when you have been sitting on black asphalt for at least an hour with shaved heads and no hats, but I digress. Sitting there as the drill sergeants were calling out names and places, names and places, for an hour straight. Obviously, my last name starts with "S" so I was at the bottom of the list. I had been daydreaming about taking naps and watching a movie with bae (who is still bae to this day btw) when "Shotwell, Wiesbaden Germany" was shouted out.

Omg was I daydreaming? Did they really just say Germany?? *No way people actually got what they asked for in the military*, I thought to myself. But there I was, sunburned head and all, sitting on the ground in a trailer park parking lot, headed to Germany in a few short weeks. Fast forward to the final day of basic training and our "homeroom" drill sergeant brought us together for what we thought was going to be a tearful goodbye. One riddled with "atta baby", "you guys were the best group of stinky privates we've ever had", you know typical rah-rah stuff. We're all standing around waiting a.k.a. standing in formation waiting one last time for some heartfelt words from the people that have ruled over us the last 5 months. Joy is overflowing from everyone because we finally get to get out of here. Our homeroom drill sergeants walk out and they are joking around with each other, joy overflowing from them too because their jobs weren't exactly a cakewalk the past 5 months either. They are probably mostly excited that they get to go get some rest before the next batch of stinky privates step onto that black asphalt.

We snap to attention, then they give us all words that wrapped up basic training beautifully. This formation was right before getting in the car with our families that were taking us out into the free world and the three of them said "Seriously don't try to contact us . . . ever." Hahahaha's rang from us in the crowd. *Silence* "No, but really don't even type our names into Facebook. Get the fuck out of our faces. Dismissed" And that was that. We turned around, got in our cars, and drove off.

No hearty handshakes, no throwing of our berets like when you graduate school, no phone numbers exchanged, no let me know if you need anything. No nothing. As crude as it was, that taught me that getting attached to people might be a futile act in the military. Form bonds and friendships while you're there but know that sooner rather than later someone has to leave and you'll probably never see that person ever again.

Cut ties clean and keep it moving. On to Deutschland, where beer and debauchery reign supreme. Oh, and where my roommate got run over on the autobahn.

SECTION 2

The Motherland

CHAPTER 8: "SPRECHEN SIE DEUTSCH"

"Grab a mop."

—Lazar

There I was again: a duffle bag of all my belongings in one hand and a piece of official Army paperwork on where I was going in the other. I was like a child that was flying solo and had to have their paperwork practically stapled to their clueless little foreheads. I was standing at the airport, thinking *"damn I'm really about to just move to Germany, huh?"* Excited and nervous all at the same time for what the future held. The main thing I was excited about was becoming Captain America and deploying to "go get some" as soon as I got there. Little did I know that I would definitely get some of something, just not war. After two weeks of leave (vacation) at home where I did nothing but working out, napping, and hanging with bae; I said my goodbyes, and off I went.

A restless 12-hour plane ride later I touched down in Deutschland with exactly zero actual clues as to what to do next. An Apache helicopter showing up on the tarmac with dudes hanging off the side to pick me up was definitely a possibility in my head, so that should tell you the range of possibilities that were open to me. As I stepped off the plane, I just stood there and looked around for ANYONE in any sort of military uniform or high-and-tight haircut. I was a deer in the headlights. Alone in a foreign country with zero clues. I just started walking straight, past all the delicious looking beer stands (and there's a lot of them). Should I? No, no, not yet young one. There's plenty of time for that later. Finally, there was a guy in uniform. I went up to him and he immediately said "yeah, follow me" very unenthusiastically. He could definitely tell that I was lost in the sauce with my dorky ass haircut and green duffle bag. We were walking around customs and went into a room deep inside the halls of the Frankfurt airport. He takes my paperwork and says he's going to call my unit to come to pick me up. *Ohhhhhh, my unit is going to be the one to bring the Apache to pick me up. That's cool, they'll be here in about 10 minutes or so I reckon.*

Letdown number one. They would absolutely not be there in 10 minutes. My first 2 hours in Germany consisted of hurrying up and waiting for a ride to my unknown base in a windowless room in the airport. A sign of things to come. Finally, I get shuttled out of the room, down some hallways and outside to the passenger pickup area. The guy in uniform tells me to wait until another guy shows up and then get in the car with him and head out. That was it. Those were my instructions: stand there and wait until someone kidnaps you.

Have you ever heard of stranger danger man? Damn. So again, there I was standing at an airport with a duffle bag, no phone, and you guessed it... no clue. After another 30 minutes or so of standing on the curb, an old black, two-door BMW comes screeching to a halt right in front of me. The window rolls down and immediately wafts of Axe body spray come pouring out. The driver is the driest, most unimpressed guy. He yells, "throw your shit in the back, let's go." The hatch pops on this BMW. I jam my duffle bag in there and barely shut the hatchback before I hop in the front seat.

I have a natural gift of becoming friends with anyone I come across. I am great at asking questions and getting them to open up to me. Sometimes I feel selfish because I get to learn so many different things and then take that information and apply it to my own life. As we pull off, we introduce ourselves and I start doing what I do best: asking questions.

"Home is about 30 minutes away, and our unit is a complete dumpster fire. They forgot you were even coming in today, so I was voluntold to go pick up the new guy at the airport. A.K.A. You."

I'm feeling the love already. After 5 minutes in that car, I already knew I liked this guy. We'll call him McCarthy. He was dry, sarcastic, and told it like it was. He was already giving me the rundown on who was in charge, what they were like, what there was to do around here, and tips on how to survive in the unit. Our 30 minutes were up as we pulled up to a huge gate next to an airfield. The entrance was marked with a big sign that said, "Wiesbaden Army Airfield."

"Oh shit, there's going to be fighter jets coming in and out of here from Afghanistan or something?" I ask McCarthy. I was met with a harsh laugh in my face and a "FUCK NO, dude". Oh okay, my bad. But we were here. It was time to go get my rifle and grenades and get to shooting bad guys in the face I suppose. Take me there, McCarthy, and pronto. McCarthy definitely did not take me there, or anywhere close.

He took me to a three-story square building that looked like it belonged on the eastern bloc and for a second, I questioned if I had been brought to a Russian military base. I unloaded my duffle bag and McCarthy walked me through the double doors. He told me to wait in the dark hallway outside of a closed door. He knocked, went inside, and I'm assuming told them the new guy had arrived. He eventually came back and told me to wait until they called me inside. Who are they? Is Emperor Palpatine himself in there having a meeting with Darth Vader?

Good, more hurrying up to wait. I'm getting good at standing around with my duffle bag at this point. McCarthy says he'll see me later then goes outside to join the group of guys that were standing around a picnic table smoking cigs. Are they all waiting to go shoot some bad guys in the face or something? Why are they just standing around smoking? Anyways, after 20 long and dark minutes in that hallway, I learn that there is no central heating and air conditioning in Germany. No need since it doesn't get that hot there and you can just use a radiator-style heater to heat your house. "Doesn't get that hot there" is a subjective matter. I was definitely sweating all the same while standing there in the dark hallway.

Finally, after a sweaty 20 minutes, I'm called into the office to meet my new bosses and get told what to do. During my short time in Emperor Palpatine's office, I learned that we're a stand-alone platoon, meaning there's a platoon leader (officer) and platoon sergeant (non-commissioned officer) in charge. There are about 50 of us and we all live in the same building. The building that I'm standing in. The whole encounter lasted less than 5 minutes, but I definitely had the nervous pit sweats going because

I had no idea how the military worked outside of basic training. Would everyone that outranked me just yell and make me do push-ups the entire time? Or not? I was half expecting to get punched in the face when I walked into that office, but I didn't. Instead, I was told that I couldn't do anything until I went through another in-processing. One that was meant for anyone that was stationed here in Wiesbaden.

They showed me to my room, a nice corner suite on the third floor overlooking lush German farm fields, gave me a map, and told me to show up for in processing the next day at 0800 (8 in the morning guys, come on). And that was that. Before I knew it, I was sitting in a corner room with an empty bed, wall locker, and desk. I was half afraid to even go to the bathroom because again, I didn't know what the real Army was like. Was I going to get in trouble for not asking to go to the bathroom? How does this even work? There was a little Shoppette (military term for convenience store) across the street from the eastern bloc building that I now called home. After about an hour of sitting in my empty room, I built up enough courage to walk across the street to the Shopette. I thought I should probably buy some water or nutrition since I'd been on a plane or standing around for going on 15 hours at that point.

On the walk across that street, I had my head on a swivel for any officer or person ranking above me so I could give them the greeting of the day: good morning, sir; good afternoon, ma'am. I used my courage and threw a couple out there. My first as a real soldier in the real Army in my mind. They were met with an eye roll and general disdain for hearing it for probably the 100th time that day. But hey, I'm in the Army now just saluting officers and shit. They didn't even make me do push-ups on sight. Look at me go!

I felt like I was walking in a minefield, diffusing bombs along the way on that 90-second walk to the convenience store. My head was pounding, my armpit sweat was dripping, and my shoes felt like they had concrete in them. Is this what released inmates feel like after being in prison? It must be because I felt like a brand-new baby in a whole new world. By the grace of God, I persevered through that minefield and made it into the Shoppette.

As soon as I opened that door, "America, Fuck Yeah" by Team America was playing at an 11, the Marlboro Man sat atop his horse with a burner in his mouth, Jack Daniel's was spraying from misters in the ceiling, a Marine in the back was smashing Monster cans over his head then chugging them like Stone Cold, and Axe Body spray was sprayed over anyone that came in like a drive-through car wash. This was the soldier's paradise and my eyes were as big as pizza pies. Fucking awesome. Okay, maybe I embellished a little bit there but really 85% of the store was hard liquor, beer, tobacco, and energy drinks, leaving the final 15% for actual food and water. The Shoppette knew what the people wanted and they nailed it: booze, tobacco, and energy. After standing in the doorway for a minute while I got my bearings with how awesome this place was, I finally found a nice ham and cheese sandwich and water and got out of there before I convinced myself I did in fact need a 2-L can of Monster, carton of cigs, and limited-edition bottle of Jack Daniels. On my walk back to my empty and lifeless room I was still in awe that such a place even existed. How was it possible to get all the best stuff in one place?

As soon as I was about to walk into the building, I heard a voice from the smoking area say, "Hey, you that new guy?" I was in fact the new guy, so I walked over there and was met with someone straight out of the south. He introduced himself with a thick Alabama accent as Smith while simultaneously dipping and smoking a Marlboro red. He called me baby girl and asked me what my favorite beer was. He told me he had one for me in his room and to come see him after I was done with in-processing. Look at me go; I made my first friend in the Army. I'm on a roll here. Smith will have a bigger story later, but as I was walking back inside, I remembered something I needed to ask him. I turned around and asked, "Hey, man, where do I get food around here?" He smiled that big ole tobacco smile and told me to meet him right out here at 0800 and he'll show me what's up.

It was dark at this point. I had no idea what time my internal clock thought it was and with no internet or phone that worked overseas, I had no way to find out right now. I did have the book Lone Survivor, so I started to read that. Eventually, I took a shower before falling asleep wondering how I even got here. I'm sure glad I did though, tomorrow is the dawn of a new day.

Still thinking I was going to be doing push-ups all day for anyone with a uniform on, I woke up the next day and put on my uniform for the first time in the "real" Army. I sheepishly made my way downstairs to meet up with Smith to go eat a much-needed breakfast. I found him in the smoking area, probably already on his tenth cig of the day. After he finished, we started the short walk over to the DFAC (dining facility). The only DFAC experience I had in the military at this point was in basic training. That experience involved only having only 2 minutes to eat whatever was available all while getting yelled at that I was doing it all wrong. My expectation was set pretty low: 2 minutes, you get what you get, some yelling, etc.

Boy, oh boy, was I wrong. We walked into what looked like a beefed-up Luby's. (If you don't know what a Luby's is, how dare you) A huge warehouse-style cafeteria with a line almost out to the door. I couldn't see exactly what was going on up there, but I liked what I saw already. I was starving and it looked like there were plenty of options to help me out. We finally made our way up to the "cashier", i.e just another soldier taking money. He said, "it's $1.37 and we don't give change." I didn't have $1.37 exactly so I handed him the five I did have and walked past him without even looking up. I'm assuming that change goes straight into his pocket. Chalked it up to the game.

After paying, there was about a 10-yard line up to the buffet line with pandemonium going on at a cooktop at the beginning of the line. Orders were being shouted out like Gordon Ramsay himself was back there making whatever they were making. It was all happening so fast, and I couldn't quite get a grasp on what was actually going on. It was pandemonium. Then the line moved and a spatula was being pointed right at me! Ummmm. Ummmm. I don't even know what the options are or what they're even taking my order FOR, much less what I actually want. I looked around for Smith and somehow he was already halfway down the line. He was no help. I'm burned.

I'm on my own.

I can do this.

I can order breakfast.

I am capable.

I heard people yell out EVERYTHING SCRAMBLED in the 20 seconds I had been standing there and I think I liked everything (considering I hadn't really eaten in a day). With a red face and sweat dripping down my pits (obviously), I yelled out, "*EVERYTHING SCRAMBLED!*" Of course, my voice cracked like I was 15. Everyone turned around to see me, the new guy, standing there wishing he could melt into the concrete (it's me btw, I'm the new guy wishing I could melt).

Another couple of minutes go by and I get close enough to see what all the fuss is about on that cooktop. An impressive sight of logistical and culinary majesty is what was going on. A guy was standing there in an all-white chef outfit, hat included, gold rank, gold unit badge, and formal name badge. The Chef Army guy was making no less than eight omelets of whatever you wanted, ham and cheese, everything, just peppers, no onions. He was on top of it all somehow. There were even real eggs, nonetheless! Man, this was a whole new world outside of basic training. Once during basic training, I was standing in line in the DFAC there and got to see the box that the supposed eggs were coming from. It was a white box with big blue box lettering that said, "FOR INSTITUTIONAL USE ONLY." FOR INSTITUTIONAL USE ONLY?! Us prisoners, er, recruits are getting fed a different kind of food? My brain was spiraling then and I still have to hold myself back from googling what's in "institutional use only" food. It can't be good.

Anyways, back to gold chef man. He held the fate of everyone's morning in his golden hands and let me tell you, he was nailing it. After he handed me my *everything scrambled,* I realized the great decision I had made. I was already happy and then I realized there was more food to be had! The rest of the buffet was every breakfast food you could think of...pancakes, sausage, bacon, biscuits, gravy with meat, gravy without meat. You turn the corner and there's a full salad bar of fruit, yogurt, juices, milks, and cereals.

Incredible.

I couldn't believe it.

Nobody was around telling me I couldn't have anything. Nobody was timing how quickly I was eating. Everyone was just sitting at regular tables like civilized human beings. I grabbed a bowl of fresh-cut pineapple, found Smith, and started inhaling what was the best breakfast I had ever had.

The DFAC was to be a great gathering place for me over the next 3 years. Breakfast was always banging in there and rank didn't seem to matter. I made new friends including the base Command Sergeant Major, talked about life, laughed hard with strangers, got cussed out, and sat across the table from other tired souls. You could walk in on a weekend and see everyone wearing their hangovers on their face. In some cases, they would be wearing their drunkenness while eating their biscuits and gravy. It was a Waffle

House x 1,000 there during breakfast and it soothed my soul. There was even some national news program on the TV's scattered in the sitting area. CNBC, CNN, and Fox seemed to be the top rotation. I wonder if that's still the case today?

Back to that first day: I finished stuffing my face and Smith drew on a napkin the way to the building I needed to be at for in-processing. We said good-bye and I got to walking. It was the middle of July in Germany and it was beautiful outside; mid-80s, little breeze, lush foothills all around. I was still ever vigilant and had my head on a swivel for any salutes I needed to throw up. After a 5-minute anxiety-riddled walk only following the crayon drawing I got at breakfast, I made it to the basement of a building. This basement is where I would spend the next week or so learning all I needed to know about the "real" Army in Germany. The room was filled with a melting pot of rank, gender, age, and ethnicities. All of us in uniform and all of us brand new to Germany. We learned how to speak and read Deutsch at a very basic level. We, way too easily, got our international driver's license (traffic circles and simple signs are awesome). We finished other admin items including getting our post office box, completing even more paperwork for the Army, and overall learned what was what, who was who, and what was where. The what was what, what was where and who was who part always puts me at ease in new situations so that was a nice surprise.

CHAPTER 9: CAN I BORROW YOUR CAR?

"Why are you carrying that microwave you big dumb idiot?"

—A cop to me on a road

During my time in in-processing, I learned through observation that not everyone had cars in Germany and especially not everyone on base. The military will ship your car over to you for free if you want. That wasn't really an option for me since I had sold all of my earthly possessions. Our base wasn't in a centralized location. This meant there were multiple locations, miles apart, that all served different purposes. The grocery store was 3 miles away from my barracks, which was another couple of miles away from the electronics store, which was over by the main gas station.

"So, how am I supposed to like, buy groceries and stuff?" I asked the civilian running our in-processing. To which she responded, "Oh, don't worry, there's a shuttle bus that runs from here that will drop you off at the bottom of the hill by the grocery store." Fantastic news! I was so glad to have options. Smith had told me that not everyone had a car and they all just shared cars in the unit. I didn't know anyone in my actual unit other than him and wasn't comfortable with just introducing myself and asking for a ride to the grocery store. *Nahhhh, I got this, I'll just take the bus, I got nothing else to do anyways.* So, the next day after in-processing I was waiting at the bus stop, twiddling my thumbs (pre-iPhone era kids) and thinking about life. Once the bus showed up, I loaded up and left the base that I was on for the first time. I finally got to look out the window at the beautiful German countryside. Ten minutes later, we pulled up to a bus stop at the bottom of a hill and I hopped off with a shopping list and a good attitude.

On top of my list was a microwave for my barracks room. We weren't allowed any other form of heating up our food, so the microwave was my life blood. I headed down the hill to the Walmart of military bases: the PX. It really is like a Walmart, just minus the food. It even comes complete with the type of people that frequent your local Walmart. You know the ones I'm talking about, don't act like you don't. I quickly became one of those people when I checked out with my $30 microwave and realized I still had to go get actual food from the Commissary (grocery store). The Commissary was a mile away on top of that hill I just walked down... So. Yeah.

I was the guy pushing a shopping cart up a hill in the middle of a military residential neighborhood. I obviously had no idea what I was doing so the sweat filling up my armpits was for a lot of different reasons. I finally made it up to the top, plopped my beloved microwave into a cart and got the bare essentials for a meathead that only had a microwave. This list included egg whites to chug (they're pasteurized so it's safe, lay off me), oatmeal, frozen chicken breast, peanut butter, yogurt, and a loaf of bread. Oh, and a big bowl and spoon.

Then there I was, standing in a parking lot on top of a hill, with a grocery basket full of food and a microwave. Now all I had to do was get all of this.

1. Down the hill back to the bus stop.

2. Off the bus and up to my barracks room.

One step at a time is how. Off I go, down the hill with six grocery bags cutting off the circulation on both arms, carrying a microwave in a box, barely able to see where I'm going. Obviously, sweating through my under shirt and uniform shirt. All the while wondering, what am I even doing here? I had lost the bus schedule somewhere along the way so had no idea when the next bus was coming to take me back to base. So, I just stood there at the bus stop waiting with my microwave and groceries for the next hour. Surely someone was going to see how much of a mess I was, stop and say "Hey, what the fuck are you even doing?" Nope. The bus finally comes though. I lug all of my stuff onboard and off we go.

Okay, back at the base. All I have left is about a half-mile walk from the bus stop to my barracks. As I'm loading the groceries up my arms and stumbling down the bus steps with the microwave a police car rolls by, stops, and throws on its lights.

That's it.

I'm done for.

I don't know what law I broke but probably the one about having dumb ideas.

The passenger window rolls down and a chisel-jawed dude with a big fat dip in his mouth says, "Hey, aren't you that new guy in the unit?" I look around and look behind me, bags from my left arm slide off and my yogurt goes flying everywhere. Before I could even say anything, I hear the driver yelling, "Fuck yeah that's him, get in you idiot." I got in and off we went. I got to ride in the back of a cop car for the first time in my life…with my groceries and microwave on my lap. They dropped me off out front of the eastern bloc barracks and gave me some parting words.

"Dude, just ask someone to borrow their car next time or call someone who's on shift and they'll give you a ride…dumbass."

That was my first indoctrination of the biggest thing that I got out of the military: you take care of each other. No matter if you like the person or not. We're all in this "thing" together just trying to figure life in the military out. Basically, just trying to not get fucked by the big green weenie while having a good time.

Even when I left the military, it took me almost a decade to realize that complete strangers can just take care of each other. When I joined the military, I thought that looking out for your fellow soldier, marine, airman, or sailor meant saving their life in battle. That was the only way it could work in my mind. Until I got continuously picked up by those strangers when I needed someone. I eventually learned that we don't need combat and we don't need a uniform. Caring for each other can include just asking "Hey man, can I borrow your car?"

CHAPTER 10: TOBY KEITH IS MY HERO

"Gimme my M4 and show me the bad guys."

–Every new person when they show up to their first unit

The time had come, I was ready to kill bad guys. I had gone through MEPS, swore in, sold all my stuff, partied in Vegas, went through basic training in a trailer park, moved across the world to Germany, and went through in-processing. Nothing else is in the way. Just give me all my combat stuff and let's get me out there. The playlist in my head was the Go Army commercial's music and Toby Keith's "American Soldier" on repeat. All I had to do was go to sleep, wake up, meet my actual unit, get my weapons, and get going . . .

No.

Nope.

Not even close.

The next morning, I woke up ready to take on the world. With the sun shining bright. Hmmmmm, weird I'm supposed to be up at 0530 (morning), with the sun nowhere to be seen. So why was it all up in my face like this? I laid there for a good minute trying to get my bearings about what was even happening and that's when the anxiety kicked in. I very nervously began to turn over and looked at my alarm clock. I was hoping that my biggest fear wasn't true. Please, please, please be a dream, a warp in time, something to do with time zones, maybe the speed of the Earth or something. Anything but oversleeping on my *actual* first day in the Army. The day I was for sure going to get all of my cool guy gear and head off to war.

With one eye half open I finally willed my body to turn over and look at the alarm clock. 0730?!?! Oh my god. I almost fainted. My life flashed before my eyes. This can't be real. I threw my thin blanket and pillow across the room so fast they almost flew out the window. I practically jumped into my PT (physical training) shorts and t-shirt. After dry shaving like an animal, I was out the door in less than 2 minutes from the time I saw my own life flash before my eyes. I was beet red, sweating already, and spiraling as I locked my door behind me. I was spiraling just like at MEPS when my roommate told me he was drinking beers behind the dumpster. I was for sure going to get kicked out of the Army before I even got to shoot one single bad guy.

After I fumbled my way into locking the door because my hands were shaking so bad, I started sprinting towards the stairs with no plan in place. I hadn't even had the time to come up with an excuse, much less a viable one. I was sprinting down the stairs with my head down when I bumped into SSG Pasqual. SSG Pasqual was my very first squad leader who happened to live on the same floor as me.

Welp I'm dead. Send my belongings home and bury me out back. *Will they drape a flag over my casket?* Would hurling myself off the third-floor banister be a quicker death than whatever punishment was about to be hurled my way by SSG Pasqual? I was willing to take my chances that I would be spared. SSG Pasqual, calm as a cucumber looked up and said "Damn man, you missed your first day. Just give me a heads-up next time so I don't have to cover for you on the spot. I told them you had one last appointment today. Now just stay in your room until around noon, then come down and find me. My jaw was on the floor. I was in utter disbelief that I was actually being let off the hook and shown compassion on my first (of many) fuckups. "Roger that," was my response and I went back into my room and melted into the floor behind the closed door, just like in the rom com you're thinking of. I took the biggest sigh of relief ever and realized that the day of getting my M4 and the rest of my war gear was still happening. *Tighten up soldier.* Taking care of each other, despite rank, was being hammered into me. People in the military show up not by words, but by actions. I saw it firsthand right there on those stairs.

Noon rolled around and I came out of my room with a fresh uniform, new boots, and new pens in my sleeve. Ready to fuck some shit up. During my hide-out time waiting for noon to come, I re-read the battle scene in *Lone Survivor.* So yeah, I was pumped to say the least. I went down the stairs to the dark hallway where all the higher-ranking people hung out and worked. The door was open, so I just stood there in the hallway. Waiting. And waiting. And guess what? Yep, waiting some more. I had hurried downstairs to make it early and there I was. Standing there waiting.

The best analogy of hurry up and wait is a doctor's appointment. You rush through traffic to get there on time, maybe even earlier than your appointment. You have high hopes of getting in and out quickly. You check in with the front desk, fill out all your paperwork, then sit in the waiting room while reading a 2-year-old People magazine. You sit, and you sit, and you sit. After 18 time checks and three different magazines, you finally get called back to the back. The military is all of that minus the magazines and the apology of "sorry we're running behind" from the doctor. Oh, and usually you're standing instead of sitting while trying not to lock your knees out and fall flat on your face. After 15 minutes in the dark hallway the big boss, platoon sergeant Lopez, yelled my name in his thick Puerto Rican accent.

I was getting called into the big leagues. I was Mario Rivera getting called in to close out game 7 of the World Series. Time for war. Toby Keith acting as my walk-out music, "We'll put a boot in your ass, it's the American way." Fuck yeah Toby, let's go get our marching orders to Afghanistan or Iraq.

"Go upstairs, everyone is up there," is what I got from Lopez. Oh, okay, cool. I just stood in this hot hallway for 15 minutes to hear that. I feel like you could have just yelled that out to me, but whatever. You got it boss. Can't kill my vibes, I got bad guys to shoot. I turned right out of there and started walking back upstairs, a big smile on my face.

They must keep the arms room on the second floor. Smart with the high ground and all. Getting a gun is *the only* thing I was thinking about on my slow walk up those stairs. *I wonder if the grenades and rocket launchers were in there too? Maybe they kept those in a separate spot. Do I get them now or is that a once I get there type of thing? Oooooh, this ACOG scope is gonna be sweet on my M4. Just like in Call of Duty Modern Warfare.*

Before I got to the third-floor landing, I stopped and gathered myself. It had been a long seven months leading up to this point, but I had made it. I couldn't help but smile. I was in the Army now. Captain America was me and I was him. I took one final big breath and then looked up while giving thanks to Lord Toby. I stepped onto the second floor to receive what was rightfully mine. The Go Army commercials said so. Black Hawk Down said so. My recruiter said so. I stepped out onto that floor to 20 sets of eyes staring right at me. I was a deer in headlights looking right back at them. My deer eyes weren't seeing any M4s with grenade launchers attached to them.

I stood frozen staring back at them, blinking slowly. Was everyone playing hide and seek with all the guns or what? This was the first time I was seeing this many people from my unit in one spot and the first-time meeting most of them. I was just standing there with my mouth open staring back at them, looking for any hidden weapons that I had missed. Maybe the arms room where they kept all the M4s was behind a hidden wall. That must be it, yeah, that's definitely it. Like one of those pull a book down and the whole wall swings open type stuff. Sweet.

Sadly, the only weapons I ended up seeing were mops and brooms. I guess we're going to sweep the enemy to death? Another moment of my military experience where time stands still while I stand there dripping sweat down my sides. It felt like hours, but really was only about 30 seconds. Deer in headlights staring back at a group of soldiers who were holding a bunch of mops and brooms. I cannot even begin to comprehend that this was even possibly the military that I signed up for.

WHAT HAPPENED TO WE'LL PUT A BOOT IN YOUR ASS IT'S THE AMERICAN WAY, TOBY KEITH?! Huh?! Cause all I see is a bunch of boots standing around mopping an already clean floor. Didn't these idiots know that the enemy is OUT THERE, not on the second floor of this barracks building? Shouldn't we at least be at the range shooting our M4s? Or practicing throwing grenades or anything else but this?

Then the nail got driven into my heart by an accent straight out of the swamps of Florida, "Grab a mop bruv, we've been at it for 4 hours. Don't be shy bub." In a trance, I half stumbled my way in the direction of the swamp drawl. Then I met the person behind the drawl: Lazar.

Lazar, who would go on to be a good friend of mine, put his hand on my shoulder and said "you thought you were going to deploy as soon as you got here huh? Me too bub, me too, but we're not going anywhere, anytime soon." Then he said the words that would haunt me for some time. Words that a hoorah, Go Army commercial watching, high-and-tight havin', dog tag on the outside of your shirt when you're back in your hometown wearing, red-blooded American, been brainwashed in basic training, brand-new soldier like me would never want to hear their first day at their first real military unit.

Remember when Ralphie finally tells Santa he wants a Red Ryder Carbine Action BB gun? Where Santa tells him he'll shoot his eye then pushes him back down the slide with his boot while saying HOOO HO HO? I do! I experienced that same gut-wrenching response to something I wanted so bad. But instead of Santa delivering that blow, it would be Lazar. Instead of *you'll shoot your eye out with a boot to the face,* I got…"We're a non-deployable unit dude."

Instead of HOOO HO HO, I got a "but you'll get used to the disappointment, don't worry" as a parting gift. I turned around and just mindlessly pushed a mop around an already clean and polished floor. It felt like everyone was giving me space to process something they had already been through and accepted. Finally, Smith came over and said, "you ready for that beer now?" I couldn't bring myself to tell you when you first got in the country."

I slowly nodded my head while tears welled up in my eyes. He patted my back and said, "You got it, buddy." I spent the next 2 hours or so sweeping, mopping, scrubbing with a sponge, and mainly thinking about my life decisions. I was feeling frustrated. Frustrated that there is no possible way that we are all still up here cleaning the floors and walls of this hallway. I finally built up enough energy to ask the unaskable question when tasked to clean something in the military: "How much longer we got?"

A hush fell over the crowd and an audible gasp was let out. It was as if I had interrupted the Pope himself during Sunday mass. It seemed like a very logical question to me. It was in fact the 20th time the same exact spot on the floor had been mopped and it was definitely clean. The other inmates, er, soldiers, finally broke the silence and just started laughing collectively.

"You don't ask that question," someone said. "We're done when they say we're done," came from somewhere else in the crowd of laughter. Just another voice of the voiceless that is the inmates, er, us soldiers.

This sure is starting to feel like we're in actual prison right now I thought to myself. I decided to keep that one to myself and just kept pushing my broom aimlessly around. I had begun the slow process of resigning myself to the fact that we were actually going to be sweeping, mopping, and scrubbing this hallway for the foreseeable future. I started opening my ears and realizing that everyone around me was just hanging out. Talking about movies, music, where they were going out tonight, nothing in particular, everything in particular. Just bullshitting. That really put me at ease and I started introducing myself to everyone. I began inserting myself into their bullshitting. Acceptance through our shared suffering.

A theme in the military I learned then was "together" in a glue word type of sense. Sucks we gotta mop and sweep this hallway like a bunch of jabronis, but at least we're doing it together. Sucks we gotta be standing around doing nothing out in the cold, but at least we're all doing it together. No matter what *it* was, combat-related or not, *it* was about being together. *The glue word* was of course unspoken. Talking about your feelings is a no-no in the military. But togetherness was still there. There were shit bags up there on that second floor mopping the floor, but they were our shit bags. Don't touch them. That applies to life outside of the military too. I'm sure we can all think of someone or a group of someones that have some shitbags in them. If you can't think of a shitbag in your group, then guess what? You're the shitbag, shitbag. Have a seat over there. We look out for the shitbags though because they're our shitbags and they look out for us too. Let's face it, we're all just shitbags helping shitbags.

CHAPTER 11: SHAM SQUAD

"Actually Sergeant, AR 670-1 says that . . ."

–Proud member of the Sham Squad

Law and Order SVU opening music plays

In the non-special forces military system working too hard is considered especially heinous. In the military, the dedicated E-4s who investigate these hard-working conditions are members of an elite squad known as the Sham Squad. These are their stories. Dunnnn Dunnnn

E-4 Mafia, Sham Squad, shammers. All names from the outside, but the outside doesn't get the real Sham Squad. In fact, from the outside looking in, all E-4s look the same. It's not like we all wear pinky rings, medallions, or any other identifying marks. Nobody would tell you they were in unless they vetted you and knew you were in too. So how would you know if someone is in the E-4 Mafia? It would take some close observation and studying, but there's a way. First, they're usually in groups of two to four. Anything bigger will create suspicion. Secondly, they probably needed a haircut about two days ago, but you really can't tell because you actually don't know the exact regulation so you don't say anything. Their hair is definitely longer than yours.

When you're in "it" there are no formal names, only an understanding. An understanding that isn't written down or even spoken aloud most of the time. An understanding that is learned by seeing and doing. Actions (and especially non-actions) speak louder than any words can in the squad. These understandings have been passed down from generation to generation.

With modern beginnings dating back to pre-WW2, the E-4 Mafia has been living in the gray. They have been getting out of work and making the military gears turn for over a century. The military's official stance is that non-commissioned officers or NCOs are the backbone of the Army. But if you need something done, it's the mafia, the squad, the E-4s every time. Ask anyone that's been in the military, they'll tell you.

E-4s are the eyes, ears, and noses on the ground and in the trenches. They know everything that's going on officially and unofficially. They have spies and operatives in every unit in the military. They're who you go to if you need to know the official military law, the unwritten rules, and anything in between. They're salty, disgruntled, rarely want to get promoted, and have an overall disdain for "the man."

But you must know that not every E-4 in the military is a part of the squad. No, no, no… you must be born for the sham life. You must be willing to sacrifice praise and promotion for freedom and knowledge. You must be accepted by your peers, be trustworthy enough to not bring down the organization, and have no desire to get your stripes and become a traitor (get promoted to sergeant). You must be okay with being called lazy. You must be okay with being threatened with punishment on a regular basis. These are part of the understandings that go unsaid.

There's an understanding to never volunteer for anything under any circumstances. That's too much work. The mafia doesn't like to work anymore than we have to. There's an understanding that you delegate any and all work that's given to you. The privates are privates for a reason. They cut the grass with scissors, not you. You stand around and watch them. There's an understanding that you never nark anyone out. Regardless of their rank and regardless of if it's going to hurt you. Snitches get stitches. Do some pushups and get yelled at, you'll be fine. There's an understanding that when the time comes, we must befriend some non-commissioned and commissioned to advance our agenda and receive orders that benefit the squad. Most of all, there is an understanding that there is no short-term glory. You will be ridiculed and looked down upon out of jealousy. Jealousy of the freedom you've created through the knowledge of the rules and the game that is the military. Rules of the military and the game that's being played within the hierarchy that is the largest organization the world has ever seen. You're playing chess while everyone else is playing checkers. Time to hear stories of the chess games and chess players that I got to be a part of.

One of the hardest parts of coming up with this part was condensing the number of Sham Squad members that I write about. I could fill this entire book with the biographies of some of the great E-4 Mafia members that I got to serve with. And I likely *will* fill a book with all of their stories. But for now, we have to focus.

Tighten up on a few.

Give you a taste of what a Sham Squad member is.

Set the scenes.

Time to buckle up cause here they are.

CHAPTER 12: FRANK THE TANK

"I'm going to get us new cars."

–Frank

Frank set a cop car on fire. I just had to get it out. It feels good but hear me out, I gotta tell you about Frank as a human first.

If you're from the northeast, you probably have a Frank the Tank on your street or at least know of one. You're probably thinking of them right now and giggling to yourself because you *know*. If you're from anywhere but there, let me break it down for you. A Frank the Tank is a wild creature that you've never been around, seen, or even knew existed for that matter. The Frank that I knew and loved far exceeded any expectation that I may have had about what an asshole from the Northeast United States was like.

The Frank I got to serve with was from New Jersey and was built like an absolute tank; a 6'4" 250-pound type of tank. A 250 built on pastrami sandwiches. He always had a dip in his mouth, a habit he picked up on his deployment to Iraq. He cussed in a special type of way that really accentuated his accent. An accent that wasn't particularly Boston or New York or Philadelphia. Frank's accent was special, just like he was. A mix of all the above. He looked and acted like he was in the real mafia at some point but without the pinky ring. He just didn't give a fuck. Ever. He married a German national, had a couple of kids with her. He showed his masterful Sham Squad membership by learning the

Army HR code/law for maternity leave. I got to see firsthand the uncomfortable shit-talking from our leadership because Frank actually stood up for himself and knew his rights as a new parent. It was awesome. It was masterful on his part and he didn't come to work for like six weeks.

"It says right here sergeant," said Frank as he pointed to his printed off copy of the Army regulations laying out maternity leave. Every time, it was met with eye rolls and under-the-breath cursing, but Frank was right. It did say it right there and everyone knew it. Watching him actually stand up for himself with facts and knowledge rather than succumb to the classic military "do whatever your leadership tells you because they outrank you" mantra was eye-opening to me. That was the first time I saw someone openly defy orders and push back against someone who seemingly had all the power over them. Frank proved that we mafia members—down to the lowly private—had power and we should use it every chance we got.

One thing Frank really despised was the big green weenie: the larger military machine that chews individuals up and spits them out, without regard for their feelings or needs. Big green weenie = bureaucracy. Hating the big green weenie of bureaucracy was definitely a core tenant for our group, but Frank took his hate to a different level. If Frank got a direct order to do something, he would take his time doing it while coming up with a reason as to why that order is stupid, unethical, or a combination of both. If he couldn't find a reason, then he would just take his sweet time doing the task you gave him to do.

Despite his hate for the big green bureaucracy, Frank was super loyal to other squad members and other lowly peasants that were lower enlisted like him. He was always cracking jokes, usually at the expense of a superior. He always got good laughs out of all of us with his open hostility towards anyone and everyone who outranked him. Frank wasn't scared to give direct feedback to a high-ranking officer on something that was fucked up and needed to be fixed, be it equipment issues, moral issues, or something in between. You were going to hear about it. Frank was our mouthpiece. Yeah, he may have been doing all this for selfish reasons, but at the end of the day, he hated superiors and respected the lower-enlisted peasants like us. He was our super crass and borderline rude mouthpiece, but he was our mouthpiece and stuck up for us. Just like any great Mafia leader, if something was fucked up, Frank was going to be the one to say something about it.

My main job as a Military Policeman (MP) while in Germany was the equivalent of a cop in a medium-sized city. And what do cops in medium-sized cities use to drive around all day and night, looking for problems? That's right…we drive around in patrol cars. Our patrol cars in Germany were the sleek European version of a Ford Taurus: THE Ford Mondeo. Police cars usually have four doors and a cage that separates the front seat and the back seat, right? Correct. However, the cars we got to drive all around Germany only had one of those two things. Four doors. Frank didn't like the fact there was no cage protecting us from potential criminals that were sitting in the back seat. "Not safe," he would say. And he wasn't wrong.

Those four-door sedans got driven HARD. In the snow, on the Autobahn, braking hard, pulling the emergency brake so we could drift in the snow over some sweet jumps. We treated those Ford Mondeos as our own personal Hot Wheels and they started to rack up some mileage and issues. Those small little issues coupled with the lack of cages to protect us started to compound into a big issue with Frank. He wanted the Army to invest some money into our equipment and he didn't want to "be driving a big, huge heap of shit all around Germany." Every time we came onto shift with Frank, we would hear a 5-minute-long dialogue on how the big green weenie doesn't care about us and how we should all revolt and refuse to drive these things anymore. We were at revolution time in Frank's mind.

Then, one Monday morning at 0500 (5 a.m., newbs) it happened. News of a plan. Some inside baseball here, there are three shifts typically in any police department: morning shift, swing shift (middle of the day), and mids (overnight). Shift change is where you, well, change shifts.

The overnight shift (mids) comes and turns their patrol cars in, and the morning shift comes in, gets their patrol cars, and goes to work. This particular Monday morning, I was coming on shift and went to collect my car. The person handing their car over to me had just worked with Frank and immediately warned me, while giggling, that Frank was on one. Needing a boost of energy and entertainment to start my day, I asked, "What's he on this time?" This fellow Sham Squad member shared the infamous line that I still remember some 10 years later…

"Frank learned how to set a Ford Mondeo on fire and make it look like the car's fault. He's gonna do it this weekend on shift."

Excuse me, What? I had to close my eyes and really focus on what I had just heard. I hadn't had my 32oz cocaine-laced coffee from the Shoppette yet, so I had him repeat it. Yep, sure enough, I did in fact hear that Frank was going to set a patrol car on fire to make his point that they're unsafe and a whole new fleet is in order. *The revolution is about to begin,* I thought, *and I'm definitely going to pretend like I never heard this arson plan.* That's the Sham Squad way though. Deny till you die.

The plan spread like wildfire through the ranks of our squad. Whispers of Frank's plan circulated during breakfast, smoke breaks, and on patrol. The legend of Frank's plan was growing and he hadn't even done anything yet. We all double- and triple-checked the schedule for that upcoming weekend, making sure that we worked on Saturday and Sunday—one of the only times anyone actually wanted to work on a weekend. Saturday came and went with no word of a burned-out Ford Mondeo. *Are we actually going to see Frank set a car on fire?* was my last thought as I went to sleep Saturday night. It was like Christmas Eve as a kid. I could barely sleep with anticipation and found myself just staring at the clock waiting for 0400 (4 in the morning) to come so I could get dressed and get to work.

I finally hopped out of bed, did the whole shit shower shave thing, and started walking the half mile or so to the police station to start my shift. Did New Jersey Santa bring me a gift to warm my heart? I couldn't walk fast enough to find out. And boy, oh boy, did Jersey Santa not disappoint. I yanked the door open and strutted into our meeting room. Who was sitting there while whistling a tune and wearing a shit-eating grin on his face?

That's right, Frank the Tank himself. I take a peek around the room and see another mafia member with lips tight, shifty eyes, and a shit-eating grin. He must have been Frank's partner during the arson. *Errr alleged arson.* Oh goodness, did he really do it?

I immediately start looking for the shift sergeant—think the boss of that patrol shift—and find him sitting in the corner on the phone looking down. This is looking more promising and promising as the seconds tick by. I looked back over at Frank and he put his finger over his mouth and made the "shhh" gesture. Just then he cleared his throat and said, "Shotwell, you'll never believe this, but my piece-of-shit patrol car just up and caught fire out at one of my checks. Isn't that wild?"

"Ohhh man that's crazy, are you guys, okay?!?!" I replied with obvious concern in my voice. I wouldn't want my friend to get burned, ya know?

"Yeah, luckily we hopped out and called the station right away, isn't that right Reidy?"

"Luckily," his partner, Reidy, answered.

My eyes were super shifty at this point and I almost couldn't contain my laughter any longer. I had to leave before I blew it. I bid them farewell and left the room to get my ammo and patrol car. It wasn't until my daily stop to get my crack cocaine-laced coffee from the Shoppette that I got the full story of the ridiculous overnight shift that had just happened. It came straight from someone who was on the overnight shift with Frank. I'll try to keep it verbatim as I can remember, but just know there were pauses for laughter, disbelief, and to pick my jaw off the floor. Here goes.

Before I start, we all have to keep this secret because he could be in for real deep shit so only tell people you can trust (Sham Squad members). So yeah, Frank really did it. His patrol car is out at a security check right now with black smoke all over the bumper and side fender. He wanted to figure out a way to make it look like a complete accident instead of just lighting a match and setting it on fire himself. He really did research and looked at the engine parts dialogue then went on the dark web and started figuring out what would happen if he took off certain hoses or did certain things to the engine to make it catch fire. I guess he found this manufacturer's concern that if a certain part of the exposed fuel line came loose and popped off that it would start spraying gas everywhere. That was his red herring—he figured if he could take that part of the fuel line off and start revving the engine to create a spark, then boom. Exposed gasoline + spark from revving the engine = fire. That's how Frank's brilliantly fucked-up brain works. Anyways, he knew that the weekend would be best because nobody would be out at the security checkpoints (note: we had security checkpoints that were away from the big military base out in the middle of the German countryside). *So, he got 3 patrol* (the one with the most security checkpoints) *and went out there and did it. I guess pulling the hose off and revving the engine enough times worked and a little fire started. He let it go just long enough to have a little smoke damage then pulled out the fire extinguisher and put it out. Called it in with a panic to really lay into the whole "he felt unsafe" thing and another patrol got sent out there to pick him up. Base leadership and our leadership are up at the PMO* (our police station) *trying to figure it all out now and I heard they might just recall all of the cars. Can't be having their troops rolling around in cars that just randomly catch fire, ya know? I think it might actually work; if we keep our mouths shut, we could all get new cars.*

After some skepticism by our leadership that included interviewing Frank and those that were on shift, he was absolved of any wrongdoing. Apparently, the powers that be found out similar information: If a certain hose came undone and the engine was revving then a spark could be created forming a small fire. How could Frank know that?? Riiiight?! How could he sergeant? That's crazy ;) ;)

We were told to not talk about it anymore. They said it wasn't Frank's fault and we didn't need to be joking around about it anymore. Joke's on them. They didn't need to know that the joke was that they actually believed it was an accident. Until now, but the statute of limitations is up anyways. So just have a laugh about it if you're reading this.

As for where Frank is now? I don't know because I can't find him on Facebook, which isn't shocking. I bet he's cussing someone out right now over feeling slighted. "You just don't talk to people like that Shotwell. I don't care if we're in the Army or not." Wise words by a wise man from Jersey, who just happened to set a car on fire to prove a point.

CHAPTER 13: SMITH

"Wanna go to Irish?"

–Smith, every day

Smith got run over by a car on the Autobahn. Again, sorry, just had to get it out before we go any further. Don't worry, he lived, but it was bloody.

Smith is the OG Sham Squader. He taught me what the squad was about and where I would turn if I ever needed guidance in the way of shamming. Smith was from Deep South Alabama and had the drawl to go with it. He called people baby girls and liked to play some dorky conquering game on PlayStation 3. I think he was pretty intellectual, but I only thought that because he read big sci-fi books and played that game that seemed to need strategy to play.

He was my roommate for a little bit in the barracks so I got to know him pretty well, considering we had to share a 10-by-10 room together for almost a year. Smith loved Jack and Coke, and I do mean loveddd. He was definitely a part of the Newport and Bud Light crowd. The crowd that could not work out at all, eat terribly, drink a ton, smoke cigs, and still do well on a PT test. A different breed that I got to experience up close and personal in that barracks room of ours.

Like Frank, Smith was not scared at all to speak his mind to leadership. I got to witness the many times he said, "This is fucking bullshit, sergeant." I can hear his southern drawl now.

Ironically, he and Frank hated each other. They each thought the other was a piece of shit. Hilarious.

I was such a rule follower when I was in the military that it always made me uncomfortable f when Smith would yell at a sergeant, but it also entertained me so much and I got used to it. I looked up to guys like Smith who could just speak their mind and not give a shit about repercussions. "Because I said" was never a good enough answer for Smith; you better have a good explanation for asking him to do something if you were in a leadership position. Common sense was a must around Smith. If what you were saying didn't make sense, you were definitely getting the classic Smith line of "that's just fucking stupid."

Our military base was about a 10-minute drive down a little Autobahn from the nearest town called Wiesbaden (pronounced VEESbaden). To go out for a night on the town or just experience a normal human existence outside of a military base you had to take a taxi or drive yourself. As you know, not everyone had a car and those that did definitely didn't want to drive when they planned on drinking the devil's juice. DUI's = bad in the military. If you wanted to go out to a bar or club in Wiesbaden, the preferred option was to jam as many people as possible into a taxi. Once you got "downtown" you had some options. You could go to the local bars or clubs where you would be one of a few Americans, if not the only one. You could also go to the military bars where Americans are the majority and there are very few locals there.

Smith's favorite, along with a ton of other Americans, was a place called Irish Pub. It was exactly what the name suggests. It had a couple of different rooms including an upstairs with a bar on your left when you walked through the thick wooden doors. They had a few German beers on tap, but they definitely knew what their clientele wanted- stiff and easy mixed drinks. Drinks that American soldiers would buy by the half dozen for the whole crew.

Irish Pub is not a place for mixology and trying the latest and greatest in mixed drinks. Irish Pub was/is a place you went to in order to get hammered with the boys, maybe pick up a date, and maybe beat up on an Airforce guy. It played the hits: Jack and Cokes, Crown and Cokes, vodka Red Bulls, Jager bombs, Irish car bombs, and shots in plastic cups. These were (and still are) the Irish Pub's bread and butter.

Smith just so happened to love the same bread and butter that they were selling. The two were formed in (un?) holy matrimony. The marriage was consummated by five to ten Jack and Cokes. Smith visited his bride any chance he got. If you ever want to check it out, here are the directions that are still burned into my brain. You get dropped off on the outskirts of what's known as "downtown" on the corner by the Doner kebab shack. Turn right and go down the street; Irish Pub will be like the second or third place on your left. It had and probably still has sticky floors and smells like beer and bad decisions. It is exactly what you would imagine an Irish Pub is like, except fill it with American soldiers.

We know the preferred method of getting to Irish Pub from our base is the taxi, but let's talk about the options you have when you leave there after a couple of beers and Jager bombs. No matter how shitty the situation is or how badly you may dislike or not connect with the people with whom you're serving, you look after each other. We know this much is true. This is especially true as Military Policemen (MPs) because every other person in the military fucking hates us anyways. We're called pigs, snitches, narks, battle buddy fuckers, etc.- all those names. We had to stick together and take care of each other so nobody could ever hold power over us. Selfish reasons? Sure, but still have to take care of each other. If we messed up and got a DUI or assault charge, then all those words become true. Then "they" win. Right or wrong, our MP unit had a bunker mentality: fuck everybody else, we're all we got.

With all that being said, one of the main sources to get back to base for us MPs after a night out of drinking was in the back of an MP car. First, you had to know who was "on shift" at the time. "On shift" meant who was asleep in a cop car in a parking lot somewhere. I mean on patrol as an MP at that time. Once you figured out who was on shift, you had to hope that someone in your group had enough prepaid minutes on your flip phone to make a call. If someone does, you give that person on shift a ring and ask them if they can come pick you up. You work it out then go get a doner kebab and eat it while you wait. Now these MP car pickups weren't designated just for the squad members, no, no. You could be picking up your boss, your boss's boss, or another shammer. Sometimes there might even be a companion that would have to be negotiated for. We're not running a brothel service around here and the gate guards are gonna have some questions. In

Germany, the gates to the bases are guarded by German national contractors. Come on, we MPs have *some* standards after all.

Back to the fateful night Smith got run over.

It started as a standard, stay till last call, get *almost* blackout drunk kind of night at Irish Pub. Smith went through the standard operating procedure laid out above for getting a ride home by an MP. He failed with one crucial step though, he didn't have enough prepaid minutes on his cell phone. See, this was 2010 and the smartphone as we know it today hadn't quite made it into the mainstream yet. There were a few people that had an iPhone but most of us had little prepaid phones. To be able to make a call on your phone, you had to go to the Shoppette to add more minutes. It was a whole deal, set up like early cell phone packages where even text messages counted towards your total. No prepaid minutes? No calls or texts can go out. That simple. You're always playing Russian roulette on whether a call or text can go through. On this night, Smith played the game and lost.

Okay. No big deal, he can just grab a taxi, right?

Nope, spent all his cash on Jack and Cokes.

Okay. No big deal, he's with a group of people that he can hop in a taxi with, right?

Nope, they left already and were under the assumption he was getting a ride back in an MP car.

Okay. No big deal, he has a debit card that he can use.

Nope, public transportation was shut down for the night and taxis didn't take cards in 2010.

Shit. It's 0330 (3:30 in the morning).

What to do, what to do?

Walk.

Yep, we're going to walk the same route home as the one we took here. That 10-minute car ride will take me a couple of hours, but I'll grab this Doner Kebab and just start humpin' it. Let's do it.

That's probably how Smith's drunk brain sounded trying to sober up and make a decision. He knew he needed to get itself out of this situation and make it home. So, he does exactly what his brain tells him to do. He grabs a doner kebab, pays with his debit card, and just starts walking.

He makes it out of the downtown area and is presented with a choice. He can take either the paved hiking trail that runs parallel to the Autobahn going to our base or the shoulder of the same Autobahn. The hiking trail runs parallel to the Autobahn and has beautiful green rolling hills stretching miles on either side. There are some twists and turns along the way, but the trail takes you right to the front gate of our base. So, there's that option. The other option includes just walking on the shoulder of the Autobahn the entire way; walking up the exit and walking down the service road until you get to the base.

Smith's choice that night? Fuck it, walk on the shoulder of the Autobahn where the "recommended" speed limit is 130kph or around 80mph. Recommended is the key term. It's 4-something in the morning and pitch black. There are not a ton of streetlights on this stretch of the Autobahn. And it's going great, the doner kebab is doing its job of sobering him up while also fueling him during this athletic endeavor of walking on the side of an interstate toll road with no highway patrolmen in sight (the German equivalent at least).

Absolute madman. There's a walking path right there, bro! Despite the stupidity of his decision, he made it all the way to the little exit that puts you directly on the access road that leads to the front gate of our base. There weren't that many cars on the road since it was so early, so he should have been home free. Another 15 to 20 minutes of walking and he would be tucked in tight to his side of our 10x10 room.

He would end up tucked in tight, but in a much different way than planned. As Smith was walking up the slight incline on his exit, no doubt starting to revel in the fact that he could see the lights of the base and was home free, a car appeared and decided to take that same exit as him. Just like in America, the shoulders on exits are nonexistent because you just don't need to pull over on the short exit ramp. You can just wait till you've already exited to pull over or pull over before you even exit. Exit ramps are just one-way streets with no shoulders; they have enough room for a car and that's it. There's not enough room for a car AND a human. A human is now having to walk on the actual white line because it's rocky and swinging their doner kebab bag around the side of their body. Combine those things with the lack of light and how early it was in the morning—meaning the eyes behind the wheel were probably a little sleepy—and you get a bloody disaster.

The car was going an estimated 60 mph when the passenger side mirror and front fender clipped Smith's left shoulder and arm. The impact immediately took him off his feet and spun him around, landing him on the side of the shoulder on rocks and loose gravel. The driver was definitely freaking out that they just possibly killed someone walking on the side of the Autobahn. They got out and ran over to find Smith face-down on the side of the road.

I couldn't imagine the terror going through their mind when they first walked over to find someone face down on the side of the highway. As they're stepping closer to Smith, he shoots up like the Undertaker at WrestleMania. Can't kill him that easy! He's got that Menthol and Bud Light blood running through his veins. In his case Marlboro Reds and Jack and Coke, but you get it. The driver rushes over to this bloody mess of a human and tries to render first aid. They try to help Smith up so they (the driver) can call an ambulance to take him to the hospital. To no avail. In classic American fashion, Smith pushes the driver away while yelling at him in English to get the fuck away. The Undertaker is then up and running towards the base. The funny thing now is that Smith decides to use the trails that we talked about earlier that weave their way through the countryside to get you to the front gate.

Stunned that such a creature can get run over by a car and then get up and take off running, the driver calls the local Polizei (German police) to report an opposite hit and run. Like a regular hit and run, but I accidentally hit someone and they are the ones that ran off. Must have been pretty confusing. The Polizei, in turn, get a hold of our military police station and the search is on for the unknown American that got hit by a car. The description included a large person with blood everywhere, last seen running somewhere toward our base. In classic governmental style, the call doesn't come into the right people until about 45 minutes after Smith got hit. That 45 minutes gave him plenty of time to make it to the front gate, get scanned into base, find our room, and pass out/fall asleep unseen to anyone but the local contractor who was working the gate.

It's 0500 at this point and the hunt is on for an American that got run over by a car on the Autobahn. The MPs on shift, the heroes that they are, are searching through the countryside on that half-mile stretch from the exit to the front gate to no avail. Searching all around the base in alleyways, door stoops, and dumpsters. Asking people getting out of taxis if they've seen any trace of a bloody mess walking around anywhere. Nothing.

Then the big break comes. Someone asks the gate guards if they've seen anything and one pops his head out of the shack and says, "oh yeah, he saw that drunk guy Smith come through with blood all over his face and clothes about an hour ago." I know you're probably wondering what I was wondering. *You didn't tell anyone about the bloody American soldier that looks like he got hit by a truck? When the gate guard was asked the same question he said,* "It didn't look THAT out of the ordinary. You guys come in bloody all the time, plus he said he was fine." Fair enough. But the hunt was now on for Smith.

Up until this point, the facts of the story were all straight from Smith or another MP who was on shift that night. Now we're going to pick up where I come in and have firsthand knowledge.

There I am, fast asleep because it's the weekend and I don't have to be up for another 3 or 4 hours. I'm probably dreaming of bench presses, protein shakes, and bae back home when I get awoken from my slumber by a very loud banging noise. As I start the slow process of opening my eyes and coming back to consciousness, I realize that the loud noise is my barracks room door getting kicked in. I'm wide awake now and hear screaming from the other side.

"SMITH, OPEN UP IF YOU'RE IN THERE. WE'RE GOING TO BREAK THE DOOR DOWN!"

I scream back, "I'M COMING, I'M COMING!" I take the four steps to the front door and frantically unlock and open the door for the mystery person on the other side. It wasn't just one person. It was a half a dozen of my fellow MPs blowing right past me to Smith's side of the room. *What the hell happened and what did Smith do this time* was all that was running through my head. This one seemed a bit more serious than the others. I turned and looked over to his side of the room and that's when I got my first glance at Smith.

There was a pool of blood on the floor next to his bed, a pool of blood on his mattress next to his pillow, and his hair was matted down with blood on one side of his face. *Oh my god, had I been sleeping 3 feet away from a dead person?* The other MPs were yelling his name and shaking Smith's legs for what seemed like way too long before he finally opened his eyes. Much like my reaction, it took him a second to realize six MPs were looking down at him. It then took another couple of seconds to yell out in a hungover, groveling, classic Smith voice, "What the fuck do you dipshits want?" Okay, whew, he's okay and not dead. If he can cuss a sergeant out, then he's seemingly fine to me other than all that blood.

The sergeant in charge of the goon squad that came blasting through my door shot right back at Smith, "You got run over by a car trying to walk back to base you dumbass. We thought you were dead." The air kind of got pulled out of the room on that one, I let out a Sheesh, but the kind you inhale on instead of exhale. After a quick exchange of Smith arguing that he was fine, he stands up out of bed with the help of one of the MPs. That's when everyone first got to see what someone looked like after they got run over by a car. He looked like Two-Face from *Batman*, but all the way down the left side of his body. His pants and shirt were torn, there was dried blood all down his rib cage, and road rash on his hip area, his hair was matted down, and it was not obvious whether there were broken bones or anything yet.

"We gotta get you to the medic, and now", were the next instructions from the MP in charge. They hurried him out of the room while halfway carrying him because it seemed like his whole lower body on the left side wasn't working properly. Leaving me standing there in disbelief.

One of the MPs that were in the room stayed back to get my statement on what happened. It was a quick one: I know nothing, I was asleep. //statement (police lingo for "I'm done talking"). With nothing left to discuss, we both went back over to his side of the room to stare at all that thick, dark blood that was starting to dry on the floor. It looked like a crime scene, and I wondered out loud who was going to come in and clean that shit up.

I got my answer a couple of hours later when Smith came limping back into our room– looking like he got hit by a car. He hopped in the shower to clean all the blood off his body and out of his hair. After the shower, he started cleaning everything up himself. I gave it about 5 minutes before I let out a "Soooooooooo, what the fuck happened?" He told me nothing was broken, but that he had a concussion (duh). He continued to share that the medics cleaned up all his wounds and road rash. He said that leadership was just glad he wasn't seriously injured or worse. Oh, and that he was going to rehab, starting tomorrow.

And that was that. He slept most of the day and then played his conquering video game until the next morning. Then was off to rehab for the next six weeks. I had no idea that the military even had a treatment option for substance abuse, so it was pretty cool to see him get the help he needed. Once he got back, he was the same ole salty, Sham Squad Smith just sober. He might have actually cussed out more sergeants than before since he had a clearer mind sans alcohol. He and I got a few more months living together before he PCSed (permanent change of station) and moved on to Ft. Drum, New York. We didn't keep in touch after he left and the last I heard he is married now with a couple of kids.

Such is life in the military. You form bonds and relationships and then someone gets moved to another base and that's that. Don't worry, Irish Pub was able to survive after Smith got sober. There were dozens of other drunk soldiers waiting to make bad decisions there; there always will be. I checked and Irish Pub is still alive and well a dozen years after Smith got run over.

My group of trailer kings and queens, circa 2009. Can you pick out the sugar babies?

A king with his babies. Notice we got to actually ride a bus instead of a cattle trailer that day.

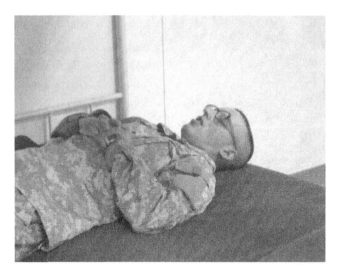

Practicing the art of sleeping anywhere. My bunk in a trailer, circa 2009

Lots of complaining probably happening on this 1,000% humidity Missouri morning.

Don't lock your knees, don't lock your knees, don't lock your knees. Hurry up and wait, circa 2010

My rock, the never changing DFAC. With one of the infamous omelet makers doing what they do best (in white). Photo Credit: (US Army)

Our patrol car: THE Ford Mondeo where naps, fires, taxi services, and debauchery were born.

The commissary a.k.a. our grocery store. The hill I lugged a shopping cart up with a microwave in is just to the left.

CHAPTER 14: NAP TIME

"That's a great spot to take a nap."

–Every cop you know

Now that we know a few of the Hall of Fame Sham Squad members, let's learn about some attributes that make and mold a regular ole soldier into an elite Sham Squad member.

We'll start with a PSA: If you ever see a cop car pulled over in an obscure parking lot or way off of the side of the road where you can't even see who's inside, I've got some news. They're not working, they are napping. Yep, full-on sleeping. Seat cranked all the way back, eyes closed, radio on loud in case they get called, dreaming of sweet nothings type of sleep.

This type of sleeping should be put on a resume. It is an acquired military skill first developed in basic training when sleep was a commodity. You have to learn how to sleep in a HUMVEE for 10 minutes at a time while you're waiting in line during training. You learn to catch a few minutes sitting up against a tree while everyone else finishes lunch. Anywhere and everywhere is an opportunity for a quick nap. If you're in a leadership position and in charge of MPs or any police unit, this chapter is probably going to make your blood boil. Sorry 'bout it.

This information is not a guess or a bold statement. I've been one of those people before. Plenty of times actually (sue me). I've been in a patrol car rotating who gets to sleep and who gets to play lookout and handle the paperwork. I've taken a nap in broad daylight on a pile of logs at a range before, in full battle rattle: helmet, vest, the whole getup.

As an MP, it's just what you do when you're working an overnight shift during the week and there's absolutely nothing going on. There are no cars on the road, nobody getting in domestic disputes, no DUIs because everyone has to go to work the next morning, and no radio chatter. The security checks are done and you've walked the neighborhoods, so what do you want from us? We're tired. We never get full nights of sleep because life happens during the day and that is when we are supposed to be asleep.

Sleeping while on shift as a military police officer can't just be done all willy-nilly—no, no, no, this is a job for a squad member. A true professional E-4 Mafia member knows that you have to use your network of fellow shammers to learn of hiding spots that only we know. A hiding spot that sergeants don't know about yet. Only a rookie makes the mistake of not scouting out locations that won't get you caught by your boss. These hiding spots have been around for generations and, hopefully, those same spots carry on today.

There are a couple of different perfect hiding spots for a nap while on patrol; these go for military police as well as regular police. The first type of nap spot is about complete concealment. You can't be seen from any road and there are no approach opportunities by foot. This type of nap spot is definitely off the beaten path and must be first vetted by another member. You have to be able to trust that when you're asleep, nobody is going to run up on you or be able to see you and snitch on you. You have to turn your radio all the way up. This way, if something does happen and you're actually needed you can snap to it and respond. MPs are held to a higher standard because we're looked at as snitches, so everybody is looking to snitch on us any chance they get. If anyone else in the military caught us sleeping, we would never hear the end of it from them or our own leadership. So that's the first type of sleeping spot: completely hidden where nobody could possibly see. Now close your eyes and go to sleep, sweet prince.

The second type of nap spot is about being in a semi-open spot that looks like you're doing something. This is the one that you drive by every day and tap your brakes because it *looks* like the police officer is running radar trying to catch people speeding. If you see a patrol car in a parking lot facing the street, off the side of the road a little bit too far, or under a tree somewhere; there's a good chance they are taking a little cat nap so just keep on speeding by. These types of nap spots are more brazen than the first and definitely a bigger gamble because you're out in the open. They can be made easier if you happen to have a partner that day and they can act as a lookout but if you're solo, you're taking a risk. This out-in-the-open nap spot has gotten more than a few of my fellow shammers in trouble. One of those people was when a fresh new private tried to jump the line and join the Sham Squad.

Brackeen had been working the road with us on patrol for about a month. He was building up his confidence every day and trying to work his way into mafia. Being out on these streets with us for a month wasn't enough time to trust him, but he was determined to join despite his rank and seniority. One day during the day shift, he decided to take matters into his own hands and tried to prove himself. He tried to find his own nap spot where he wouldn't be caught by anyone, the squad included. That's why you're not ready, young Brackeen. Thinking you can do this on your own was his first mistake. Doing it during daytime hours was his second one; that is risky business even for an experienced Sham Squad member.

Day shift on the weekend was the equivalent of the overnight shift during the week: nothing was happening. Everyone was still recovering from the previous night, spending time with their family, and/or traveling around the local area. The point is, there aren't many cars out on base, especially not the housing area Brackeen was in charge of patrolling that fateful day. A couple of hours into shift, he decided to pull over on the side of a one-way street along a curve and "run radar." He's off to a pretty good start so far; the curve along the road is a smart choice. The curve is an awkward angle to turn your head and look at the person sitting in a car because you have to be paying attention to the curve in front of you. However, the mid-day, out-in-the-open nap spot is still risky, no matter how good your setup is—and he had a good one. One of the best in fact.

First thing first, if you're going to be that close to the road in the daytime then you have to look like you're actually paying attention and doing something. How do you look like you're paying attention on such a bright, sunny, German day? You throw on the darkest-tinted Oakley sunglasses you can find, of course. Next, you're going to need to actually look like you're doing something related to being an MP. What do MPs typically do when they're sitting in their cars during the middle of the day? They run radar, of course. They are trying to catch people speeding so they can use their blue flashing lights and pretend the ticket they're going to write to people speeding is actually worth something.

Don't worry, not only are the tickets pointless and hold no consequence but the radar gun used to write those same tickets isn't actually calibrated to give a correct speed. It was all fugazi. How does an MP look when they are running radar? Well, the radar gun is usually propped up on the side mirror with the window down, that's how. Brackeen knew all these things because he had been taught how and had seen us running radar out of pure boredom. He really wanted to prove himself and crack into the Sham Squad, so he devised a plan to show all of us that he was ready for the big leagues.

After running radar for a little bit in his napping spot on the curve of that street, our sweet baby Brackeen started to get a little heavy-eyed and decided it was go-time. He dug into his backpack that was in the back seat and pulled out a small roll of black duct tape. The same color black that happened to match his black tactical gloves that we were allowed to wear as MPs. That's when he put his left hand around the handle and carefully duct-taped his own hand to the handle of the radar gun. Back out to the side mirror the radar gun goes. His left hand is now semi-permanently tagging along. Black tinted Oakley's on and head leaned up against the pillar next to the driver's seat to appear like he was "looking" at the radar gun.

It was a brilliant, well-thought-out plan that actually allowed young Brackeen a full-on nap of an hour or more. He just forgot one rule of taking a nap while in a patrol car: you always turn your communications radio up very loud in case someone is actually calling for you. You have to be able to answer so you don't throw out any suspicion. Also, you gotta at least do your job when someone asks you to. It was a rookie mistake. We knew he was fucked when he didn't answer the dispatcher's calls. They kept trying to get ahold of him over the radio net. After the third or fourth time Brackeen didn't answer, the shift supervisor went on the hunt to try to find him and catch him slippin'. It didn't take long because he was out in the open, right on a main road going through one of the housing complexes.

Going all the way back to basic training, punishment in the Army can be cruel, unusual and hilarious. It is mostly all three at the same time. In this case, the shift supervisor rolled by Brackeen on the side of the road and noticed no movement at all coming from his car despite him seemingly staring directly at the radar gun. No arm twitch, no head turn, no small recognition wave at the other patrol car. He had made himself Bernie from *Weekend at Bernie's*. The shift supervisor made the block, parked his car a little bit down the road from Brackeen's, and started walking up. He hopped right into the passenger seat and called in a walking patrol over the net for Brackeen. It wasn't Brackeen's voice though, so we knew a troll was going on. After another minute or so Brackeen's perfect plan was over and he was woken up with a soft whisper from the sergeant saying, "You're fucked."

About an hour later I was cruising around the housing area, actually halfway doing my job, when I saw Brackeen out in the distance walking on the sidewalk. As I got closer, I noticed that he was holding a radar gun – odd. As I got up on him, I rolled down my window and called out his name. He turned and waved at me with his left hand that had been duct taped to the radar gun 100 times over. He told me he had to walk the rest of the shift with it on and at that point, I rolled my window up and drove off. I couldn't laugh right in his face, so I saved him some dignity and got out of there. He did have duct tape radar gun hand after all.

At the end of the shift, we were all gathered around by our shift supervisor and were told how Brackeen got busted taking a nap. The sergeant told us that none of us better be taking naps, to which we all responded with "whooooa that's crazy! He just slept on shift sergeant? We would neeeever!" We said it while looking Radar Hand Brackeen straight in the eyes the whole time while slowly shaking our heads at him. The squad members were shaken after Brackeen got busted, for all of 48 hours. Then we were back to counting sheep on the overnight shift. Oh, hey shift supervisors, we know your ass sleeps on duty too. It's fine, just know that we know.

In the wise words of Dom from the greatest movie franchise of all time (fight me) *Fast and Furious*, "Granny shiftin' instead of double clutching like you should. You never had me, you never had your car." Translation: He wasn't ready.

CHAPTER 15: UNSECURED.
UNATTENDED.

"Whose is that?"

–Someone in the military who's about to steal your shit

Somewhere, right now, on a military base on Earth, there is a member of the Sham Squad, E-4 Mafia, or dirtbag in general that is saying out loud, "unsecured, unattended; means it's mine now." We know the squad loves to live in the gray area of rules and "unsecured, unattended" is definitely a misty gray color. Unsecured, unattended becomes a major part of the big enterprise that is the Camo Road. As a reminder, the Camo Road is the military's version of the Silk Road. An underground, decentralized, trading and bartering platform that is run by a bunch of middlemen–in this case, the Sham Squad or E-4 Mafia. Whatever you could ever want or need was available on the Silk Road, and now the Camo Road.

As a reminder, from the basic training part of this book, I was so confused why the drill sergeants always harped on having everything you own locked up. We couldn't understand why we had to lock everything up at all times. *Was the enemy going to break into our trailer park and steal my tan undershirt and helmet?* Turns out you learn very quickly when you get out into the "real" military, the one outside of basic training or boot camp, that half of that statement is true. Yes, someone does want to steal your tan undershirt, helmet, and any other thing that literally isn't nailed down. It is free game if it isn't locked up, engraved with your name on it, being actively watched by someone or GPS tracked. There is a hoarder mentality that weaves itself into the military culture and basically creates a nameless, faceless culture of sticky fingers. Why not have another laundry bag or tan t-shirt in your size? The "unsecured, unattended" phrase is a specialty of ours and one that gives power to the people of the squad.

Much like an actual organized crime unit, the mafia preys on those in need and generates its power by having special products or services. Maybe you're going to a military specialty school where there's a packing list and you're missing that one random green laundry bag or you only have the green magazine pouch but your unit is making you all have the camo one, but the store is out of them. What are you going to do? You need that camo magazine pouch because you don't want to get yelled at, berated, and made to feel like a huge piece of shit. Well, you're going to start knocking on doors in the barracks asking if anyone has that fucking camo magazine holder. You know who's going to inevitably have one? Shamsters, that's who. Yeah, but how do they always have an extra of that one random thing that you need? They acted as a human lost and found, except they "found" it while no one was looking and took it as their own.

Even more confusing is when your payment is refused and they just give you that random thing you need, like the camo magazine pouch. But isn't power derived from the money you get from people that are in desperate need? No, no, no, you've got it all wrong. When you give that person something they really need and bail them out of a situation, they owe you. They owe you big. You may not collect on that debt right away and it won't be something as easy as bumming a cig while you're out drinking. No, no, no. I'm gonna need you to cover my entire shift for me so I can have a 3-day weekend. Interest must be paid on your debt's young ones.

Once I got to my actual unit in Germany, I was quickly indoctrinated into the "unsecured, unattended" way. I was taught how to leave your nervousness at the gate and just pick up that jacket that's just lying there with nobody around. "If you don't grab it, somebody else will," was the phrase that stuck with me from the beginning.

We're going to touch on some hot spots for unsecured, unattended things. Now you too can gain power through hoarding trivial military equipment.

Here are the places where you'll be most successful:

1) Ranges

I first learned how to grab something unsecured and unattended at a range. Ranges are prime-time property grabbing for a couple of different reasons. First, there is a very large number of people there from lots of different units. That means you can really lay on the nameless, faceless, victimless crime justification. You don't even know the person that left their shit lying around! Second, ranges are pandemonium. People are running around everywhere, gotta get from one place to another, everyone has a weapon, most people don't want to be there, how you shoot on the range is directly tied to your promotion status, and there are always new people standing there like deer in headlights.

All of that combined means there's an edge in the air. Yelling, confusion, ahhhhhhh, move over there, now over here. Despite all of that, there's an opportunity for those skilled in the craft of being calm in the chaos to thrive. Insert a salty member that can calm themselves, open their eyes and ears, and float through the range instead of getting swept up into the madness.

Within that calmness, you can start to notice that people get hot and start to strip their layers before they go on the firing line. And what do they do with those layers they don't want? Well, there's no time to take them all the way back to the building they started in, so they just throw them down on the ground in a panic. They don't want to lose their spot in the sea of people trying to qualify at the range. Then they're so elated that they shot well or so anxious that they didn't, that they completely forget about whatever piece of gear they had thrown on the ground 30 minutes prior. That's where you come in, hot shot. You may be finished, or you may still be waiting your turn. Either way, you're always close to the firing line; standing there shooting the shit or casually strolling along. Calm in the chaos.

A group of people comes off the firing line and you see the jacket or the extra magazine pouch still lying there on the ground. You make a mental note of its location and give it another hour or so. You walk around a little bit, find another shamster that you've never met before, and get a feel for what they're going after that day. We all have our eyes on something. Shooting well and qualifying is an afterthought to us, we already know we're gonna do that. It's about the real prize, the camo magazine holder, a nice pen, or a jacket if you're extremely lucky (and you've warded off the other mafia members). After that hour of bullshitting around, you finally start making your rounds. You go back to the spots where you've mentally set markers of things that are "unsecured and unattended."

You're going to have some misses; people can calm down and realize they left a piece of their gear somewhere and go back for it. That's fine, don't get discouraged if your first piece of gear isn't there. Keep going down your treasure map, there will be something there for you. Stay strong. Ranges bring out everyone's performance anxiety and most people will let that anxiety overcome them for the whole day. Even when they're done shooting, they're going to be completely exhausted from having high anxiety for the past couple of hours. That's when you're going to find that jacket, that magazine holder, that med kit.

When you do find that thing someone left unsecured and unattended, are you going to rush up to it, look around, and ask someone nearby if it's theirs before you grab it? ABSOLUTELY NOT!! You're going to casually walk up to it like it's been yours the whole time. Grab it, put it into one of your cargo pants pockets, and walk back to joke around with your friends. It is worth it when you remember what that random camo magazine holder you picked up off the ground means. It means somebody at some time is going to owe you. Bigtime. It could mean an extra day off, a carton of cigs, or a fifth of Jack. The world is yours!

2) Physical Training areas. Actual gyms and unit PT areas. In that order. Being able to secure something unsecured and unattended at an actual gym is typically reliant on weather. Typically, units in the military do their physical training outside in a grass field, which we'll get to as a place of opportunity for unsecured and unattended things. Once the weather is too cold, too wet, as a change of pace, or they're just the Airforce, units will take their training inside to the big gym. When this happens, you'll be able to find sweaters, jackets, pants, Camel Backs, water bottles, shaker bottles, oh my.

In the military, next to nobody is excited to be doing physical training with their units. We either want to do it on our own at the gym or not do it at all because it takes up precious drinking time. Either option means we really don't want to be doing push-ups and jogging at 0630 (6:30 a.m.) −before the sun is even up! That disdain is there every day, it never goes away, and it is unit wide. The grumbling never stops and neither does forgetting to pick up your sweater or cool expensive water bottle. Getting out of unit PT is priority number one. If you can't get out of it, then getting out of there as fast as possible when it is over becomes priority number one. With that rush of people getting away as fast as possible comes a great deal of things getting left behind. That's when we lurk behind for an extra 5 minutes before rushing off to breakfast. All you gotta do is stay back and pick up an extra shirt or something. Yeah, it'll be sweaty but nothing a washer and some Tide can't fix. What does having an extra PT shirt mean that's not even your size do for you? That's right, it gives you power.

Starting your treasure hunt of unsecured and unattended stuff at ranges and physical training (PT) areas will start to perfect your ability to find things and understand the level of power it might be able to wield for you. The military always says you have to crawl before you can run, and in this case, you have to be able to master the basics of "unsecured, unattended" at these areas before you can branch out to harder ones. It took me a couple of months to get to where I could even notice unsecured and unattended things, let alone process if they were worth it or not. Once I did, I was ready to run.

A part of our jobs or "mission" as military policemen (MPs) in Germany was to drive out to all the closed-down military bases spread across the area we were in and make sure everything was still okay. Some of the bases were 30 minutes away and some were more than an hour away. "Make sure everything was still okay", was quite the arbitrary thing when the mission was first explained to me. Everything is okay… like how? Like all the buildings are still standing? Like there are only a few squatters living in the buildings? Like all the grass is overgrown and roofs are caving in, is that okay? Yes, to all of those questions was the answer I got. We were supposed to make sure nobody is living out there, that the fence doesn't have holes in it, and that's about it. What that actually meant to us MPs was that we got carte blanche on old abandoned military bases. It was awesome, creepy, and scary.

There is one particular abandoned base, that I won't name probably for security reasons who actually knows, that was out in the middle of nowhere. It was twenty minutes from the nearest town and even then, that town was tiny. If it was in America, there wouldn't even have been a Walmart within an hour. It was *that* far out in the middle of nowhere. This base was huge, too. There was family housing on it, a grocery store, a gymnasium, a bowling alley, and cold war missile silos; all abandoned. Anything and everything you could want on a military base, this place had it. This base had been shut down around 5 years before, so it was a creepy old ghost town by the time I got to it. The grass was overgrown, there was moss on the buildings, there were some abandoned vehicles left behind, and nobody was in sight. There was no electricity throughout the entire base and every door was left unlocked, so we had free reign to explore old buildings…if we dared. Obviously, we dared. We had guns and a can-do attitude!

Most of the buildings were completely empty, except for some graffiti and a creepy little squatters' apartment someone set up. One of my counterparts did end up getting quite the scare after having to chase the squatter away one time when they were going through an old military housing building there. Overall, it was like playing Resident Evil on PlayStation: we would "break in" to the old, abandoned buildings, pull our guns out, and pretend like we were clearing the building. We all knew that nothing was ever going to be in any of the buildings, but it made us feel high speed, so why not? The old school buildings were always the creepiest. That building never got much attention because we were scared of a little zombie kid popping up and eating us or something. The buildings were frozen in time since everyone had just left all their stuff and just didn't come home ever again.

One of those buildings became a rite of passage for us Sham Squad members that were well-versed in the unsecured, unattended world. That building was the bowling alley. The bowling alley on this particular abandoned military base was like a time capsule from the '90s. You can close your eyes and see it. The carpet with neon patterns, the concession stand sign with the white block letters, and the neon beer signs around the bar. If you try hard enough, you can even smell it in there. The smell of feet, popcorn, and sticky floors from all the spilled beer. For whatever reason, the military didn't take anything out of there when the base shut down. Everything was still in there down to the used bowling shoes on the counter. It was extra creepy and made you start thinking if you were in some kind of M. Night Shyamalan movie. The kind where people just disappear without a trace.

To add to the creepiness, there was one single light bulb over the middle of the bowling lanes that always flickered. None of the lights turned on when you flipped the switch except that one and none of the outlets worked either. For some reason this light was the chosen one. We always guessed that light was powered by all the bad decisions made there in the '80s and '90s. The bowling alley had a bit of an urban legend going around our ranks. Ghost sightings, the sound of pins falling, and the fresh smell of popcorn were just a few of the stories people would tell to exacerbate the legend of the bowling alley.

Then one day after work, a squadster gathered us around and threw a bag on the ground like we were in a Martin Scorsese movie. He proudly told us to, "check that shit out". We all looked at each other like there was going to be a finger in there or maybe a head. We shook our heads and started walking away. We were definitely not about to fall for whatever it was that this dude was trying to do. Like a toddler telling you to smell their finger-it's just best you don't. He called us back, "Wait, wait, wait, fine, fine, fine" and said he would do it, "bunch of babies." I definitely stood back at a distance —safety first. He slowly unzipped the bag all dramatically and slowly pulled out a bowling pin…from THE bowling alley. We all went oohhhhhhh shiiiit and dapped him up. He had really gone out there, braved all the ghosts, creepiness, and whatever else was going on in that bowling alley, and snatched up a bowling pin. "Unsecured, unattended right?" he said as we were all acting like a bunch of impressed 10-year-olds at show and tell. That bowling pin instantly became a Sham Squad trophy and status symbol.

Over the next year or so, a dozen of us would make the journey and pluck a bowling pin from the grasp of Satan himself. A few of those being a rite of passage for membership into the squad. When you walked into someone's barracks room and saw a bowling pin, you knew you were safe in there. That they were a real one. The bowling pin was the only distinguishing membership "thing" that squaders would display. We're petty and silly, what do you expect?

The bowling alley conquest would continue for a couple of years after I left Germany but would sadly only continue in oral history after the base was handed back over to German control. I wonder if their police or military created trophies out of bowling pins there too? Probably not, they seem way more sophisticated than us apes.

Unsecured, unattended stuff is everywhere. You just have to be in the right mindset to get it.

As a disclaimer, this whole chapter is alleged. Some might see it as theft, others as an opportunity. I'm just telling you like it is. Don't sue me, bro.

Chapter 16: Peak Performance

"You want a menthol before this run?"

–An E-4 at PT right now

I was already obsessed with working out before I ever knew that I was going into the Army. As a kid, I was very skilled and athletic but always the skinny kid. I got bit by the gym bug in college and became a gym rat. Working out as part of my job in the military was definitely an attractive part of why I enlisted and I was excited to have a bunch of workout buddies once I made it into the Army.

Leading up to basic training, I ramped up my workouts to another level. Lifting weights in the morning, running at night, and doing push-ups and sit-ups in between. I didn't want to be incapable during basic training or once I got to my first unit. I *definitely* didn't want to be out of shape when I was ruck marching through the mountains of Afghanistan shooting bad guys in the face. So going into basic training, I was more than capable of doing anything physically that was asked of me. Pull-ups, push-ups, sit-ups, carrying stuff…you name it I could do it.

I'm going to pause real quick because as I just wrote that I realized that it may have come off as overconfident, cocky, or just plain assholeish. This whole section may come off as that to some, but I assure you that is not my intention. Those push-ups, pull-ups, and other stuff I could do impressed nobody. It's not like the drill sergeants pulled me aside and made me special forces right there on the spot. So relax, it's just some push-ups, everyone had to do them.

Because of all the movies and TV shows I watched (my DVD player wore out *Generation Kill* and *Black Hawk Down* on repeat) and books I read (*Delta Force, Kill Bin Laden* got worn out), I had the expectation that everyone in the military, regardless of if they were special forces or not, were going to be physical specimens. I believed that if I didn't get into the best shape of my life then I was going to be the weakest link that would let everyone down. When I got to basic training, I was ready to prove myself physically at any moment.

My expectation was that I was going to be doing push-ups on that bus the first time I even laid eyes on a drill sergeant. My anxiety about being the weakest link physically kept growing by the hour as we kept doing stuff during in-processing that didn't involve physical activity. Days went by and I hadn't done a single push-up; just got yelled at instead. That wasn't good enough in my distorted brain. I wanted to "get some" and wear the badge of honor you get when a drill sergeant yells in your face. I wanted them to make me do hundreds of push-ups at a time. I wanted to rip the Band-Aid off and make sure I was good enough to be here. So, just like in prison movies, I would do push-ups and sit-ups next to my bunk at night. I even concocted a way to do a row/bicep curl variation on the underside of the bottom bunk. Another, obviously obsessed, guy even showed me how to do "prison" squats with someone else on your shoulders like a barbell. He said his uncle was in prison and showed him, but I'm not convinced it wasn't him that was the one in prison.

Then the day finally came during in-processing–we had our first group punishment. We were all sitting around a large assembly area just sniffing and drinking hand sanitizer so we would stay awake. A fresh drill sergeant came and had the time that day. He didn't like the way we looked and probably had never made anyone do push-ups before. So, there we were, in the front leaning rest position (top of the push-up) getting ready to hopefully do 1,000 push-ups. I was relieved. Let's get this out of the way so I can feel something again, man.

That's when I had my first realization that not everyone was Captain America in the military. It broke my heart a little when we were all at the top of the push-up, still yet to do any actual push-ups yet, and people were trembling. Guys around me were already having to go down on their knees and rest. *What is happening around here?!?! How did you even get here if you can't even hold a plank position for more than 20 seconds?* It may have not been the healthiest thought I could have had, but at that moment I was thinking, *Ohhhh noooo, how does this even happen? I'm definitely not going to have dozens of workout partners.* They're too busy putting hand sanitizer under their eyelids. Fuck.

After about 45 seconds of equally disgusted words, the drill sergeant finally made us start actually doing the push-ups. After about ten, I knew that I wasn't going to be the weakest link. I realized that I was going to be more than capable in this crowd. A weight was lifted, but I was also disappointed in those around me. *Who comes to the military unable to do even ten push-ups?* Not mad, disappointed. Just like you continuously disappoint your parents for years to come, I too would be disappointed by the lack of physical competency in the military at large.

I would continuously have to wrap my brain around how someone couldn't manage to do one pull-up when it was their job to be able to do a pull-up. Insert a push-up, a sit-up, or run a mile in less than 12 minutes into that job equation. Who let you sign your life away and raise your right hand to swear to defend the Constitution without first checking that you could at least do some push-ups? It was a strange concept to me but luckily the military also brings in absolute freak specimens that defy the laws of working out and living a healthy lifestyle.

There must be a genetic mutation that allows certain people to be able to rip darts, drink beer, eat gas station taquitos, and also run a 5-minute mile, do 100 push-ups, and 100 sit-ups. These same people then go eat biscuits and gravy before calling it a day. Lucky for me, this part of the book is not made up and I got to see it with my own eyes. Plenty of times.

For those that don't know, the Army PT (physical training) test is done usually once every 4 to 6 months and consists of three separate events for a cumulative score. The three events include: two minutes of push-ups, two minutes of sit-ups, and a two-mile run. There's rest time in between and your score can help or hurt your life in the military. If you get a high score, you're typically chosen to do cooler stuff, go to cooler schools, skip out on group PT, and go to the gym on your own. Overall, you just get preferential treatment. What really mattered though was not failing. Failing meant you were going to draw more attention to yourself. You would have to do extra workouts, have your meals monitored, and other general annoying stuff. Stuff that nobody, and I mean nobody, wanted to do. You would think that with the threat of having to do stuff you don't want to do and treated like a child, preparation would be high. That everyone would make sure they studied for the test they already knew the questions to. If you thought this, you would be wrong. Most people relied on sheer will, hope, prayers, and in some cases freak genetics to pass the PT test. It was an example of procrastination at its finest. It was like in school when you didn't do any homework or study at all, but you were shocked and appalled that you didn't pass the exam.

When PT test day rolled around, you could feel the anxiety in the building. The shit-talking was hilarious with classic favorites such as, "Are we REALLY going to take this PT test?" and "This shit is stupid." Shocked that anyone in leadership would actually go through with something that had been happening and hadn't changed since WW2. As a side note, Army get your shit together and change the PT test. It's 2023; we should know how to train our bodies to be soldiers better than this.

The first time I got to experience the most entertaining genetic mutations was the very first PT test at basic training. It was, and possibly still is, the most mind-bending thing I had seen while in the military. For someone like me–who trained hard, took care of my body, and watched what I ate and drank–to see someone who looked like they rolled out of bed, drank a beer, smoked a cig, and stumbled over to the PT test completely destroy everyone was mind-blowing to say the least. Everyone is nervous at the first PT test. Nobody had ever taken one under these conditions before (tired, malnourished, etc.).

We did the push-ups and sit-ups in the parking lot of the trailers, obviously. That part wasn't really all that shocking to me as I had already seen people failing to do more than five push-ups during in-processing. Those people weren't going to be able to magically do 50 more push-ups in 2 weeks. I had already come to terms with that. The run part is where I learned that people are just built differently though.

Leading up to this, we had collectively run maybe a couple of miles since being at our basic training unit. I was actually a bit nervous that I had fallen out of shape since I got there. I wasn't a naturally spectacular long-distance runner, so I was worried all of those nights of running back at home were wasted. After the push-ups and sit-ups, we walked about a mile over to a trail that was designated for the run part. We stood huddled around the start line with everyone's feet marching in place out of anxiety.

Then we were off. Over a hundred of us running down a trail in the darkness, not knowing where we were headed. We only knew that there was a turnaround point somewhere out there in the abyss. We just had to keep running hard and boy, oh boy, some of us could run harder than others.

Halfway to the turnaround point, I saw ten or so of the most malnourished-looking troops in the whole company go blazing by me headed in the opposite direction. *How is that even possible?* That thought stuck with me until after I came back and crossed the finish line. *How could it be that anyone in the Army could run that fast at all? Shouldn't they be running track in college or professionally? How could they run that fast while eating McDonald's every day?* None of that group of ten that blazed past me in the opposite direction looked like they knew a single thing about nutrition or training. Not one! My mind was in a blender.

Maybe what I thought was the best way of training wasn't the best way of training at all?

Maybe I shouldn't be so uptight about what goes into my body? Maybe I should just start smoking and eating McDonald's?

Maybe then I could run a 5-minute mile?

Maybe all those chicken breasts and broccoli were pointless and actually holding me back?

The dagger in my heart occurred after that first PT test when I went up to that infamous group and asked them what their training was like leading into basic training. *How many miles a day were they running? Did they do any sprint work? What about weights?* The blank look on their faces when I asked followed by a giggle was all I needed to know. With a deep southern accent, one of them said "Shit man, I ran cross country in high school but that was years ago. I didn't do nothin' but drink beer before coming here." If there was a pillow around, I would have screamed into it.

"So, you're just naturally able to run a 10-minute 2 mile?" I asked.

"Yeah, I guess so," he answered with a shoulder shrug.

Now it was my turn to give a blank stare. I stood there staring at them like they're all alien species. I could not compute. I continued to be blown away by this Newport and Bud Heavy breed every single time we ran long distances or took a PT test. After the second time it happened, I justified it by telling myself that they're not currently smoking cigs and drinking beer every day. Being clean, sober, and younger than me is obviously what gave them a 2-minute-per-mile advantage over most people, myself included.

I believed everything I had read and watched about training hard, eating well, staying away from drugs and alcohol, and becoming a physical specimen as a result.

Well, that ridiculous hypothesis was quickly debunked within the first 2 weeks at my unit in Germany. I quickly realized that everyone really hated taking PT tests and just wanted to be left alone. Most didn't want to have to do any physical training at all in fact.

During basic training, I was holding onto false hope that once I got into "the real Army" more people would be like me and want to work out in their free time. I just wanted us all to be Captain America, man. During those first 2 weeks in Germany, I was going to the gym by myself, but was justifying it by telling myself that I was the new guy who didn't know anyone. I was just delaying the inevitable. Less than five other people in my unit ended up ever going to the gym on their own time and NO ONE, and I mean NO ONE, wanted to do group PT in the mornings. I became acutely aware of this on my first day of unit PT. This is where everyone is *supposed* to be together to do push-ups, sit-ups, runs…you know, Army training stuff.

That first day we had PT, I walked downstairs and there were only six of us dressed in the actual Army-issued PTs. Everyone else? In regular uniform with an excuse as to why they couldn't do PT that day. Having an appointment was the most widely used and accepted excuse. If you were upper management—a senior NCO or any officer—you didn't have to give an excuse at all. Just a "got stuff to do" sufficed for those guys. Seems like the six of us ready to work out were the only slubs that forgot to have an excuse.

In that moment though, our leadership told everyone that we had to take a PT test the next morning. It was like a flash back to basic training. You would have thought that leadership personally slapped everyone's mother in the face. The GALL. The AUDACITY of them to make us take a PT test. The bitching, moaning, and anxiety were in full effect for the next 12 hours. During the test the next morning I got to see some leadership maybe, potentially counting by twos on their friend's push-ups and sit-ups. I maybe, potentially saw some leadership get cycled to the back of the line and their PT test scorecard get filled out by Harry Potter's wand or some shit. Everyone saw it and that made the barracks HOT with bitching and moaning the rest of the day. The bitching, moaning, and conspiracy theories from the leadup to actually taking the PT test were now justified so it was all ramped up to 1,000.

After the push-ups and sit-ups, it was time for the 2-mile run portion of the test and ours happened to be on an actual airstrip. We were all huddled around an access gate waiting for someone to come unlock it when the Newports and Camel Crushes started coming out. The people filling the air with a minty smell were the same people that "had appointments" anytime we did group PT. People I never even knew smoked were lighting up and that sweet, sweet smell of menthol was filling the air. I was offered a dart from at least eight different packs. When I declined, I was told, "Bro, you know menthols open up your lungs right?" by one guy. Another included, "Yeah, yeah, yeah, right before you go on a run if you smoke a menthol your lung capacity is higher so you can run faster." Now, I like to think I have my Ph.D. in Broscience but the menthol cig increasing lung capacity was a brand-new idea to me. I had spent a ton of time down rabbit holes on the internet reading forums (Reddit and bodybuilding.com are peer-reviewed right?) and never read about the causation of menthols. I passed on all the Newports and stood back and watched everyone around me chain smoke until the gate opened. *Well at least I know I'm going to smoke these dummies (pun intended). They just got done getting cancer and I've never once seen them do physical activity. See you idiots at the finish line.*

That's right, I would see them at the finish line. They were all waiting for me, finishing off their menthol heaters. The definition of smoking and joking. Not even out of breath. My original hypothesis about the Newport and Bud Heavy crowd was shot down and completely false in every way. These people were older than me, outranked me, smoked cigs seconds before we ran, and drank beer every night. I could only help but smile. These were the salt-of-the-earth type of guys that I actually wanted to be like. I didn't want to be all polished and perfect like Captain America. I wanted to be like the dudes in WW2: smoking cigs, drinking whiskey, and fighting. That military is romantic to me and I got to experience it firsthand every time the word PT was mentioned. Conventional wisdom, when it came to workout performance, is thrown right out the window when military people are involved. Cigs, alcohol, gas station food, energy drinks, and can-do attitudes propel soldiers to run 5-minute miles.

If you were to try to force them to get sober and start a workout and nutrition plan, you would take away that dog inside of them. They would fall flat on their face and become injured, lose motivation, and get slower. I saw it with my own two eyes. Those Newport and Bud Heavy people taught me a valuable lesson: I needed to lighten up. I needed to not take myself so seriously. I needed to not hold my own beliefs on how things needed to be done in such high regard. At the end of the day, there are people out there that are hungover and smoke Newports before an Army PT test that can run a 10-minute 2 mile. You'll never know about them. They get no accolades, no medals, and no praise. They do it so they can be left alone. The gig's up now though. If you smoke menthol cigs, drink beer every day, and don't work out, you'll run a 5-minute mile. That's the real secret—not giving a fuck.

SECTION 3

THE Unit

CHAPTER 17: AIR ASSAULT. AIR ASSAULT. AIR ASSAULT. AIR ASSAULLLLT

"Oh, you wanna be high speed huh?"

–Someone mocking you for wanting to do something cool in the military

As a result of that first PT test, I did loosen up my expectations for what soldiers in the military were going to be like. I realized that everybody is different, just like in the real world. Not everyone was a gym rat like me and that was okay. I got humbled by the old crusty Newport crowd and it allowed me to not take myself so seriously.

One thing I definitely took advantage of was the weight that a high PT score carried. If you scored high enough on a PT test, you all of a sudden unlocked a certain type of freedom. You could be trusted to work out on your own outside of designated group PT times, not that anyone was actually going to those anyways. Another perk of a high PT score is getting chosen to go to sought-after schools. In my non-deployable unit's case in Germany, that meant anything "high-speed." Let's define high speed because it can be cringe in the military TikTok society we're living in. High-speed is what my expectation going into the military was: running and shooting, jumping out of planes and helicopters, shooting bad guys in the face, having the best gear, and looking cool while you're doing it. It's being G.I. Joe. As we know by now though, I was in a non-deployable unit. This made us a bunch of G.I. Nos instead of G.I. Joes. Since we weren't going to sniff combat anytime soon, going to these schools was the only way we were going to get to do any of that "high-speed" stuff.

You may be thinking, *oh that's cool you can just sign up and go jump out of planes, or just show up to sniper school, or dive school, or air assault school.* That would be too easy, people. That would make too much sense for the military. Come on, don't be ridiculous. No, no, no. You had to be approved and chosen by another adult human to be able to go learn a new skill. And, you guessed it, a high PT score was the top indicator on whether you were going to get picked for those high-speed schools everyone wanted to go to. You could be an actual criminal, but if you have a high PT score, you got preferential treatment.

We touched on a few of the top high-speed schools you can attend in the military above but didn't mention that the number of people who can go is regulated. The military decides how many people can attend throughout the year. Once they have the total number, they designate a certain number of "slots" to the different branches, MOSs, and units within all those branches and MOSs.

In my 3 years at this non-deployable, detached platoon-sized unit in Germany, I saw one high speed school opportunity make it all the way down to us. Rightfully so, those slots needed to go to people actually going into combat. Those troops needed to have those skills. We non-deployable folks just wanted to do cool stuff for once. It was a depressing realization when I realized I wouldn't even get to play pretend for a few weeks every once in a while.

This time was different. We had the chance to try out for the opportunity to go to Air Assault school. Big time excitement all around. Hold on, it's not that easy. Not only did we have to go somewhere to TRY OUT to even get a slot, we first had to get past everyone else in our unit. Only three of us from our little platoon of goons were even able to try out for a chance to get one of the slots. This was going to be the best of the best Newport and Bud Heavy crowd and I ended up being picked as one of the three to go try out. I was super excited–this was my chance to feel alive–to get even an inclination of high speed. To see how the Army actually operated. This felt big time to me and the other two guys that got picked for tryouts.

As it mostly goes in the military, we got told we were chosen the day before tryouts. That meant zero opportunity to get ready physically and a short window to prepare mentally. One of the least fun things about going anywhere on the military's dime is the packing lists. No matter where you go, if the military is sending you there, you need to bring a whole list of very specific things. Not just any ole duct tape, duct tape that's a certain color. Not just any underwear, tan underwear and seven of them. Not just any amount of pens or paper. Four black pens with clear centers and two pads of college-ruled, spiral notebooks with red covers. No joke, those are real things on packing lists.

The lack of notice combined with the very specific list of items makes for a stampede of anxiety the night before you're supposed to leave to go anywhere. Inevitably, you never have that one thing off the list and the store where you buy that stuff is typically closed. That leaves you to scrounge, borrow, and beg to get that one unmarked green laundry bag that you needed. If you found one to borrow, that now meant that you'd owe someone. The likelihood that you would actually use all of those things you stressed so much about was always very low. It was a classic military game of do exactly as I say even though everyone knows it doesn't make any actual sense.

Once my bag was packed with all the unnecessary items, I caught a couple of hours of restless sleep. I was excited to get to at least sniff out something high speed. I couldn't help but keep playing the scene in *Black Hawk Down* where they repel out of the helicopter to go save their fallen comrades over and over again. I was like a little 10-year-old boy every time I watched that scene. Dust was kicking up from the blades, the soldiers were hanging their feet off the side, and they were wearing cool goggles. *Damn, that could be me!*

The official military definition of Air Assault is "the movement of ground-based military forces by vertical take-off and landing aircraft"—such as the helicopter—"to seize and hold key terrain which has not been fully secured, and to directly engage enemy forces behind enemy lines." Are you serious, bro?!?! I was back being Captain America when I learned I got to try out to do *that*. Learning how to repel out of helicopters, tie up cargo that would be picked up by helicopters, tie up cargo being thrown out of helicopters, anything involving stuff or people going into or out of helicopters. I was maybe going to do that?! You also get to wear a cool helicopter badge on your uniform and everybody loves a cool badge on their uniform. Much high-speed.

The other two guys that were chosen to go to tryouts were just as pumped as me. We were the chosen ones to go sniff some high-speed stuff from our small little outpost platoon of misfits. We knew at least one of us had to make it through tryouts. We had to prove to everyone–not only in our little unit but outside our unit– that we could do cool stuff too. The three of us had finished drinking our coffee from the Shoppette. We chose to drink the brew that was called JOLT; I swear it had cocaine in it.

If you have inside information as to why the JOLT brew had 10x the caffeine in it, holler at me. Anyways, we finished our coffees and were just staring at each other while waiting for our ride, no one wanting to state the obvious. I finally fluttered my eyes, took an out-loud breath, and said, "Weren't we supposed to leave 20 minutes ago?" Another out-loud breath by Sgt. Davidson, one of the other chosen ones, "Yeah, man." We were disappointed ALREADY because waiting there for a ride by our platoon sergeant played right into the belief that our unit was a mess. No wonder we didn't get to do cool high-speed stuff, someone always fucked it up. That's just the military though. Let down after let down. Expectations crushed.

We were keeping a positive attitude this morning though. We were about to go sniff Air Assault School! Nothing can hold us down, especially since we had JOLT running through our veins. Sure enough, a couple of minutes later our platoon sergeant showed up in the Sprinter van that's going to carry us to the promised land. That's right, we had Sprinter vans as our throw-around military vehicles before they were cool. Peasants. We all got in and prepared for the 45-minute drive ahead of us to Battalion headquarters, where the tryouts are happening. We were all buzzin' on the way there. We blared music while talking about how cool it would be if one of us got to go to Air Assault school and repel out of a Blackhawk. We were a bunch of excited kids signing up for the Army all over again. The excitement before becoming callous to what the military is actually like. Before this non-deployable unit. We were basically living in *Black Hawk Down*. We were also sharing all of our nervousness by wondering what the tryouts were going to be like. We knew we'd have to at least take a PT test, run some sprints, and climb a rope a couple of times.

Will we have to do land navigation?

Will we just be doing push-ups and sit-ups all day long until people start dropping?

Will it be last man standing type of stuff?

Do we have what it takes?

We had been living the high life by being basically cops for the past couple of years. Could we be high speed for a day? We ruminated then went back to listening to Lil Wayne while replaying how sick it would be to slide down that rope from a heli. Just a couple of heli boys in that Sprinter van. We were juiced up and ready to go.

There was one little thing stuck in the back of my head that made me go hmmm. Our leadership kept saying tryouts started at 0800. We were going to get there a little before 0800 no problem, that wasn't the issue. The issue was *why is something starting at 0800 in the military?* That never happens, everything always starts at 0630 or earlier. So, why was a very high speed, Hooah, go Army thing starting at 0800 all of a sudden? I didn't verbalize that little concern. I was about to but moved on when "Blunt Blowin" came on by Weezy. Can't be puttin' that negative energy out there in the world during that song. We had repelling out of helicopters to do damnit!

We made it to the base with plenty of time to spare, despite missing our jump-off time. We were even 15 minutes early. Enough time to make it to the big open field where tryouts were, get the nervous pees out, get set, and take a breath or two before the day began. Then our stomachs sunk as we pulled around the side of that big empty parade field. It appeared as if there were already a hundred or so people in dirty uniforms doing up-downs behind their big duffle bags. *Maybe this is just another unit doing special PT or something?* I didn't know this base really well, so there were probably other big empty parade fields on this tiny base in the middle of nowhere Germany. *Right? RIGHT, SERGEANT?!?!?* Our heads started to slowly hang when the only reassurance from our platoon sergeant was a very dad-like "hmmm." Nobody was about to ask the unaskable. Nobody was about to even put *it* out there that we were late. Can't do it. There's no way. *Surely, we didn't just completely miss the one opportunity our little tiny unit had of doing something remotely cool?*

That's exactly what happened. We pulled into a parking space right in front of the hundreds of mud-caked soldiers. Our platoon sergeant put it in park, took a deep breath, and told us to wait in the van while he figured this out. *Don't think there's much to figure out, sergeant...we're late.*

As soon as he got out and shut the door, we all hung our heads and started snickering like little schoolgirls. There wasn't anything else to do. It was a comedy of errors. This was our life in the military. Miscommunication. Let downs. We had been preparing for this moment, even conditioned for it. Just another chapter of the well, this book that's being written. We kept our heads down and mouths covered as we were snickering because our first sergeant was a couple of feet away from our van. Quick definition: a first sergeant in the Army is equivalent to a regional manager in a retail operation. In military terms, a first sergeant is in charge of an entire company of troops. They've typically been in the military for close to 20 years, so they've seen their fair share of bullshit. Big boss stuff. Well, our first sergeant was berating poor SFC Lopez (guy who drove us).

"How could you be so stupid to think something actually started at 0800? This is the Army, you idiot!"

Kinda has a point there, sergeant.

"You just ruined an opportunity for those three troops to actually do something high speed for once in their God forsaken lives."

Fair point there, too, sergeant.

"What a waste of fucking time for everyone."

That's what I'm saying, first sergeant.

"You can't get fucking anything right can you Lopez? Do you even try to be good at your job?"

Yikes. He's had enough, first sergeant. We'll take it from here.

No response from our brave SFC Lopez. He had no reasonable rebuttal to the tongue-lashing he just got. Us van gallery members couldn't get enough though. We had to really fight to keep straight faces as we looked out the windows. As much as we tried, we couldn't hold it together after what SFC Lopez said next. I didn't know much, but I did know that this was not the time to ask what he was about to ask. As soon as we saw Lopez's lips move, we knew it was a bad idea. Davidson, part of the van gallery, let out a slow-motion "NOOOOOOOO!" as the first three words came spewing from Lopez's mouth.

"Do you think . . ."

I yipped out a "NO! WHAT THE FUCK, NO!"

Surely, he's not going to ask the first sergeant ANYTHING. What could he possibly want?! We were on the edge of our seats, dead silent inside that van, with our ears glued to the windows. We had to hear what he was going to say. Fuck it, Lopez. Just say it. We're here for a good time, not a long time.

"Do you think my guys could jump in and still do the tryout?" he asked.

OH. Oh, no, no, no . . .

Mind you, we were now 90 minutes late. The hundred or so troops that have been there since 0630 were sweaty, dirty, and already done God knows how many push-ups, up-downs, and sprints. They've already been yelled at for having the wrong shade of underwear from their packing list. That's when the van gallery decided to look away. We couldn't watch it anymore. It was going to be too much to bear. I stole a quick glance and saw the first sergeant's head looked like an actual red balloon that was about to pop from the pressure. I saw him take a big breath in, point to the van, and calmly say, "Go".

Ten seconds later, Lopez was in the van and we were fuckin' out of there. The van ride back to our base was completely silent, the vibes killed. Not even Lil Wayne could bring the heli boys vibes back. It was like when your parents were in a fight on a road trip and you and your brothers were the back trying to be silly, but no one was laughing. That one probably hits a little too close to home for some of you guys, but you know it's true. It's awkward. Once we rolled back up to our base, we all just grabbed our bags, gave a head nod to each other and slow mo' walked away. Boy, oh boy, I couldn't wait to tell everyone in the Sham Squad. This was going to be headline news.

There's not a whole lot more that an E-4 Mafia member loves more than a juicy firsthand account of how terrible the military is. Assuming that the big green weenie is always trying to f*#k you is one of the unspoken rules of the squad. Any evidence supporting those assumptions is met with great joy. I meandered upstairs, dropped my bag off, and headed down to the smoking area to drop the news to the nearest set of ears. The three of us were back about eight hours earlier than expected, so when the group of people smoking and joking downstairs saw me, they started dying laughing. They knew. They didn't know exactly why but they definitely knew that our leadership fucked something up. If not, I wouldn't have been there walking towards them.

Lots of laughs as I recounted the story to them—red balloon face first sergeant and all. Lots of head shaking, tsk-tsking, and "Are you even surprised?" Nobody was even mad; how could you be? Yeah, I was a little let down that I wouldn't be sliding down a rope from a helicopter like a Go Army commercial. The all-seeing big green weenie had other plans for me though. Maybe it spared me so I could live to tell the tale of how I was two hours late to the only opportunity to do something high speed in the military.

Is this why a lot of us military folk have trust issues? Probably. But look at the bright side, I've learned to manage my expectations. To the point of not really having any and just picking my feet up and letting the river take me wherever it's going to take me. That's what the military is all about. There are too many moving parts not to. And isn't that what life is all about? There are too many moving parts to try to swim upriver. But the big green weenie is undefeated.

CHAPTER 18: THE BEST

"Why is the Kool-Aid Man punching me in the face right now?"

–Me, while the Kool-Aid Man is beating the shit out of me

I would be remiss if I didn't also include the *one* time my unit didn't completely shit the bed and I actually participated in a tryout for a high-speed endeavor. You may have heard of the Best Ranger competition the Army puts on every year. It's a continuous 62-hour competition held at Ft. Benning to determine the best two-person team of Army Rangers. Those 62 hours consist of physical, marksmanship, emotional, and intellectual beat-downs before a winner is crowned. Well, the military police have a similar event every year called...Best MP competition. Original, I know. It covers much of the same stuff: physical, shooting, intellectual, emotional, all of it. Now granted, the Best MP competition has to actually test knowledge of the law instead of just knowledge of the flavor of each crayon in the 64 pack like the Rangers have to know but I digress–crayon eaters.

I had already been in my unit in Germany for over 2 years at this point. I had fully accepted my non-deployable role and learned to celebrate my rank. I was just living my life, dreaming of the day that one day maybe I could do something high speed. Maybe one day the dreams I had when I went to MEPS and swore my little oath would come true. The whole being late to the Air Assault thing had happened already at this point, so I was pretty calloused to the whole high-speed thing. Then one fateful Wednesday morning I got a call on my prepaid burner phone that pulled me right back into my Toby Keith soundtrack having ways.

"There's this thing called Best MP competition and you've been picked to go try out with two other people."

"Nice! When is it? I definitely need to prepare. You know, study, do some weapons training, switch up how I work out."

"Oh . . . ummmmm; it's tomorrow morning at 0600 so we'll leave at 0500. See you then, bye."

"Hello? Helllloooo?"

They had hung up. Leaving me sitting there thinking *WHAT THE FUCK*?!? Classic non-communication in the big Army. No preparation time. "What better time than now?" I told myself and started to get amped up. I began pacing around my room—actually playing my Toby Keith playlist on Pirate Bay. I mean playing the Toby Keith music I paid for on iTunes.

The first thing that popped into my head was, what's the packing list? I was probably going to need to barter within the Squad to get the inevitable random thing that I didn't have already. So, I called back my team leader (direct boss) and asked if there was a packing list. Maybe I could get just a little more information on what I was getting myself into as well. I got a classic "call you back" line, so I went back to pacing around my room getting super excited in the meantime. Wow, I'm going to go do actual Army stuff tomorrow! No idea what it'll be, but it'll be the G.I. Joe Army stuff that I had signed up for! About halfway through watching, you guessed it, *Black Hawk Down*, my leader calls back. He lets me know the packing list and offers a very, very broad overview of the events for the next day. And by broad, I mean, "You're taking a PT test first thing then after that I have no clue." Wow. Fascinating. But the good news? There is no packing list. Wear your PT clothes and put a regular uniform with boots and stuff with weight to it in your ruck sack and bring it. This is a tryout for one of six slots on the battalion Best of MP competition with probably 50 or so people trying out. No outside food or drinks was another thing, but whatever. I could actually go to bed now instead of rushing around trying to find that one thing I was missing out of a bullshit packing list.

The next morning, we rolled out in our Sprinter van and actually showed up early to this tryout! It was a brisk fall morning in Deutschland and the three of us from our little platoon were standing out there already dreading having to take a PT test. As we all know by now, nobody, and I still mean nobody, *wants* to take a PT test. Even when it's for something cool like this. We made it to Battalion headquarters with time to spare, but we still had no idea what was going to happen next. It was to my grand surprise that when we gathered around and got briefed (talked to) by the big boss, head honcho, the battalion command sergeant major, that this PT test was not going to be an ordinary PT test. This PT test, on that dark, chilly morning, was going to have one standard across the board, regardless of your age (like normal). He broke that news after some rah-rah we have the best unit of MPs in the Army and now all we have to do is prove it part.

"Oh, by the way", he says before stepping off to go smoke cigs somewhere, "the 2-mile run will be done in your boots." He also drops that if you don't do 75 push-ups, 75 sit-ups, and run a 14-minute 2 mile, then you're done for the day and will not be able to carry on in the tryout. The upside: if you make one of the two teams, then you get to move to the battalion headquarters for 4 months to train and only train. He goes on to say those six people will have strength and conditioning coaches and nutritionists and whatever else we need to get us in tip-top shape. Now you're talking my language dude. Getting to actually work out as my job? Maybe my dream of getting to just work out as my job in the military would finally come true! I'll run around in some boots to make that happen.

"We legally have 23 hours to keep you until we have to pay you extra so this will be a long day. Buckle up boys," were his final words to us before we were yelled at to change into our boots and form lines for the push-ups and sit-ups.

Well, color me surprised that my little unit of shitbags didn't know shit about fuck and told us none of this until the night before. Not gonna back out now. I didn't know what we had to do but I knew that being able to work out for a living was on the line, so I was going to give it a good college try.

First up was push-ups and sit-ups. People were already wylin' out when they got their 75 of each. Yelling out, "SEVENTY-FIVE, SERGEANNNT," like they had already won something. I hadn't been exposed to this overinflated sense of excitement since basic training, but it kinda turned the volume of Toby Keith up in my head. "Hey Uncle Sam put *MY* name at the top of his list and the

Statue of Liberty started shaking her fist." The vibes were high even though some people weren't making it to the higher standard of 75 push-ups. Those who couldn't do it were told to go stand over to the side. Little Toby inside my head didn't care cause it was my turn. Of course, I do my obligatory 75 then watch as the sit-ups happen in the same fashion. By the time the push-ups and sit-ups are done, about a dozen or so people are standing off to the side, most already smokin' cigs. Don't feel too sorry for them though. I bet about half of them only came for the day off work or a break in the monotony that is the military. They wanted to live a little. Get out of the house a lil bit, ya know? Enjoy that heater boys and girls; you've earned it.

It's run time and you know what that means, the menthols were out in full force. Even at this tryout for supposedly the best of the best of what the Military Police Corps had to offer, the menthol cigarette still reigned supreme. Guess there's no denying that science, right? My poor, unconditioned shins and feet were already shaking in their boots. This may come as a shock to some of you, but boots are heavier and more uncomfortable than running shoes. Whatever, what's a couple of shin splints anyways? This is my chance to do something cool so go ahead and fuck me up fam. Let's run this 2-mile. Of course, the remaining 30 or so of us are standing around the start line because what's an event in the military without hurrying up to wait, a.k.a. stand around?

As we were standing there getting cold, I decided to turn to the guy next to me and ask how long he'd known about this tryout? I already knew the answer and I already had my tssk and teeth suck ready in response, but I asked it anyway. This guy looked like he was on a double dose of Adderall. He looked so American that he could be Captain America's son. He definitely had that Newport/Bud Light blood we talked about in the beginning. He was amped up and probably about to run a 10-minute 2-mile in boots. He snapped his perfectly cut high-and-tight head towards me and said, "Two months. I've never been more ready for something in my whole life." Then snapped his head back to face forward like a T-800 Terminator. "That's cool," I muttered. "I got about 12 hours' notice, soooo" my voice trailing off as I roll my eyes in the back of my head and smile a little smile. Imma just try my best, ya know?

The run finally kicks off and about 20 steps in, my shins are already feeling it. Dammit I'm such a newb. I tied my boots too tight and they're cutting off circulation to my lower leg and foot region, making my lower leg swell up like a balloon. All those times I had watched *Black Hawk Down* finally came in handy. I put myself in their boots, running out of that God-forsaken city at the end of the movie. Bet those guys were aching all over, some of them shot up. The least you could do is run your hardest in your little manicured soft-ass feet. I ended up running my fastest 2-mile ever at just below 14 minutes. My savior, Toby Keith, playing in the proverbial loudspeakers in my head. Damn right, Mr. Toby Keith, I am an American hero.

On to the next event. Feels like I have drop foot and my shins have no circulation, but on to the next event. On to the next event– meaning I have no clue how many events there potentially are. This could have been the entire tryout for all I know, but nope. We were shuttled into a gymnasium and told to change into our ACUs (regular uniforms). We were minus a few people after the run and they can be seen smoking and joking as we walk into a cold dark gym. We get in the gym and guess what we did there? How surprised would you be if I told you that we…waited around in the stands for no good reason for at least an hour? If you've been following along or have experienced one day of the military, you probably aren't shocked at all. *Genuinely what could be the holdup? Are we waiting for the bears we're wrestling to arrive from Serbia? The answer can't be anything that cool.*

Just as we're all about to settle into a nice nap position, somebody running this circus finally comes up to the front of us and starts passing out a stack of papers that are stapled together. A quick flip through those pages reveals that it's a written exam and there are about 200 multiple-choice questions with about 10 short answer writing prompts in the back. Ringmaster buddy up front tells us to spread out in the bleachers and that we have 2 hours to complete our packet. He then walks off. I open my packet ready to really dive into these questions. What could we possibly be getting tested on. Would it come as a surprise to you that I had absolutely zero clue about even the vocabulary of the first page of questions? That there was not even a chance that I had ever seen or heard any of the topics these questions being asked to me covered?

We're talking Military Police Corps history, weapon systems functionality to include bullet trajectories, maximum ranges of those weapons, UCMJ penal code, and some theoretical short answer questions thrown in there for good measure. They knew I just drove my MP patrol car around all day and night and gave out pointless tickets from time to time, right? Like what are you guys even talking about, "maximum effective range of an MK19?" The pistol I get to carry on my hip while I'm working isn't even allowed to have a round in the chamber. So, wtf you mean you want a theoretical battlefield security perimeter with flanking positions, to include different weapon systems within each of those elements? Where's the section on how to change your IP address so you can illegally stream shows from the US (allegedly)? Where's the real stuff, best of MP people, huh? Needless to say, I only needed about 30 minutes on this part of the tryout. That 30 minutes included 10 minutes of me pssstting my way down a whole row of people because I didn't even bring a pen. Great. Go me.

After I sat there twiddling my thumbs for the next hour or so we were off to the next event. We stayed in the gym and watched five footlockers get wheeled onto the gym floor. The main dude running this operation told us to listen up then explained that an entire stripped-down weapon was in each of those foot lockers. He explained that we were going to have 3 minutes at each station to reassemble them. There were a couple of caveats though: 1) we wouldn't know which weapon system was in which locker 2) they were going to turn off all the lights so we would have to do this shit in the dark. I let out an audible giggle because, well, I was a nice house cat back at my unit.

I patrolled around in my police car all shift. I definitely didn't handle the 240B machine gun every day, that's for sure. I had gotten the opportunity to shoot the machine guns and automatic grenade launcher twice up to this point. Neither of those times did I have to break it down and put it back together. It was about to be a bloodbath of tears in this gym. Hope the people supervising each weapon station were ready for me to blankly stare at them and move a bunch of parts around for 3 minutes. You can take a break on me, my boy, there won't be much to inspect when I'm done. By the time it was my turn, it went exactly how you and I both had imagined. Laughably terrible. I managed to get the M4 rifle put together enough to be respectable, but the 240B station just had its parts rattled around in the box by me—no clue where any of those went. As I got up from that station I whispered to the inspector, "Don't worry about it" as he put down a big fat zero on my score sheet. On to the next event though, fuck it.

After another 30 minutes or so of waiting around doing absolutely nothing in the stands, we got handed what's called a rubber ducky. A rubber ducky is just a fake plastic M16 weapon that has the same weight as a loaded "real" one. We were told not to lose it and then were walked over to a big cinder block square building. They put us in line and told us to wait until we heard "NEXT" called. The people putting this tryout on are really nailing the "sit around and wait" part. You guys are really getting an accurate assessment of skills needed to be the best MP. Good job. The only instructions we were given while we waited for *whatever this was* to begin, was that we had to go in and "clear" the building. Okay, I kinda know how to do that, to no credit of the Army though. I read Brad Thor military thriller novels and watched *Black Hawk Down,* so yeah, I know a thing or two about clearing a room, okay?

As I wait my turn for the next 20 minutes or so I keep thinking, *are we just going to go "bang bang" when we have to "fire" this rubber ducky weapon? Are the evaluators just going to watch how we move around in there? Wouldn't it be a more accurate assessment if we had live rounds and had a real go at this building?* What do I know, though? Nothing much is about to be the answer.

It's my turn, so I stand up and go cut the pie to the front door (cut the pie is a tactical term for moving at an angle outside a doorway). So far so good, so I put my hand on the door handle and twist it. Once I step inside, I'm basically Scot Harvath from those Brad Thor novels. For the first 10 seconds I was hookin' and jabbin'. Making all the angles, throwing a sideways gun in there, and I'm feeling good. Then out of nowhere a red flash grabs my shoulder, a little too hard, from behind and spins me around. I'm now face to face with a big red Kool-Aid Man looking thing in a huge, padded suit.

Before I could even get out a, "what the fuck?" The Kool-Aid Man punches me square in the face. Silly Kool-Aid Man. I've gotten my ass beat a couple of times while I'm drunk, you're not getting off that easy. Ole big red does have the upper hand on me though, him having a head-to-toe padded suit on and all. After a couple of minutes of fighting the Kool-Aid Man, I think I wear him out enough to grab my rubber ducky, stick it in his face, and basically run out the back door. Damn man, I didn't know I signed up to get jumped in a shitty outhouse building. I coulda set that up on my own.

Afterwards, I met up with the others who had also successfully been jumped. We couldn't help but laugh at each other's busted lips and swollen eyes. As I was tasting the copper taste in my mouth, I could see Toby Keith giving me a thumbs up. So, I sucked it up and put some dirt on it.

After everyone was done, we were thrown an MRE for lunch. You know I had to turn into the Sugar King all over again. I turned a 20-year-old into a sugar baby real quick and ate two MREs. Sue me.

On to the next event. We strapped up our rucksacks, gathered around a start line and somebody in charge told us that we were rucking an unknown time and distance. They just said to keep walking until we saw a finish line. "It's somewhere out there. 3, 2, 1, Go!" they shouted and about ten people took off running with their 50-pound rucksack. Oh boy, *do I run? Are we running? Yeah, I guess we're running.* That little jog/run of mine lasted about 10 minutes before I settled into a walking pace and being in my own mind. There were no headphones or smartwatch telling me how much longer I had. I only had my thoughts and the guy next to me if either of us felt like talking. Oh, and my rubber ducky. Still had that thing.

Nothing really to report on the ruck march, it's pretty straightforward. You just walk with 50 pounds on your back while awkwardly holding onto a rubber rifle until somebody tells you to stop. Three hours later I came across a finish line on a dirt road in the middle of the woods. Onto the next event they said, drop your ruck and walk down the road a bit for instructions. No "good job". No "this is your time". No nothing. Just walk down the road.

The sun was beginning to set, so the options are starting to get limited on what this next event could be. I followed the metaphorical yellow brick road for the next 5 minutes and what did I find at the end? Unfortunately, it wasn't Emerald City. Not even close. It was a map of the area with six points on it, a compass, an azimuth, and a 2-hour timer to find all the points. That's right, land navigation. At night, in the deep forest of Germany known as the Black Forest. It's called that because how dense the trees are. No real light can get through the trees so it's dark in there no matter the time of day. There's a theme here–I had done land navigation exactly once in my military career, and that was in basic training 2 years ago. And when we did do it in basic training, it was very rushed with minimal instruction. It was more of a nice pencil whip to get the hundreds of us to actually "pass." *Black Hawk Down* didn't have a step-by-step instructional guide to land navigation using a compass and neither did Scot Harvath in all those Brad Thor novels, so I didn't have a plan.

I was about to go walk around and get lost in the Black Forest, wasn't I? What was I supposed to do? Just hand the map and compass back to the person and say no thank you? I don't think they were offering hot chocolate or pie at the time, so I wasn't going anywhere but into the black abyss of that forest in front of me. I wasn't going to go down without a fight though! So, I grabbed my supplies and quickly turned to the person next to me and asked them how all this works. It was a genuine question from me, but a complete joke to him apparently as my question was met with a genuine chuckle and, "Yeah, this is gonna be a tough one, huh?" *Dude yeah, it's going to be a tough one. That's why I'm asking you how this map works. I genuinely don't know, sooooo you gonna show me or what?* When he saw my blank stare and glossed-over eyes, it clicked for him that I was being serious. The reality that I actually didn't know how to work any of this.

With an eye roll and a teeth-suck, he said "fine". Right there at the opening to the Black Forest, with the sun saying its goodbyes for the day, I got a 60-second tutorial on how to plot points, step count, and plan a navigation course. I retained less than half of those 60 seconds but set out with all the confidence in the world to my first point on the map.

It took me about an hour of turning around, finding different points, and stopping 50+ times to make sure I was headed in the right direction, but I did it. I found a point! The forest was so dense that you couldn't make it ten steps without running into another tree or stump. This made my straight-line planning pretty inefficient, but I was so excited to have found even that one point! Now I only needed to find five more in the same time it took me to find this one, but *hey* let's not worry about the future, huh? We live in the moment, right? I ended up finding two more points over the next hour. This made for a grand total of three, which is half of the six in case you know the taste of all the different crayons. It was pitch black by this time and all I had for a light source was a red-lensed flashlight that was flickering because the batteries were on their last leg. I was trying to find the next point when I realized I was completely lost. At my lowest point, so low that I had convinced myself that it was too dark and the military was going to have to send a search party after me. I got startled by something close by in the forest. Great, now I have to deal with fucking Bigfoot out here while I'm lost. Now the search party is going to find my body half-eaten by the black forest monster. That thought was now running through my brain as I tried to juggle getting unlost and not getting eaten by said monster. I finally just kept walking and 3 minutes later came face to face with the black forest monster.

It was a little old German woman hiking through the woods, minding her own business on a nice evening stroll through the forest. We froze, looked at each other and tried to figure out how we had both gotten here at the same time. *Was she a lifeline to me? Wait, she probably knows these woods like the back of her hand?!* I tried to break the ice by asking, "Spreken ze English?" met with an even icier stare. I didn't know what else to say alright?! *Of course, the hiker in the middle of the forest in Germany doesn't speak English. Idiot. What to do, what to do? She's gotta be able to help. I can't just wave bye and leave the only help that can pull me out of this literal dark place? No, no, no, I couldn't be lost in the woods in a foreign country and not at least show the hiker lady the map to see if she knew where we were, right?*

Shooters shoot ya know? So, I did. I showed her the map, shrugged my shoulders, and moved my finger all around my map as if to say, "Where the fuck am I, lady?" HELP ME was oozing through my body language and sad face. She stared me dead in the eyes, shook her head, and gave me a tsk tsk as she walked off. Cold-blooded! *Thanks for nothin' lady. I guess I'll just freeze to death and rot out here in these woods! Your old ass can't take those back-to-back Ls we gave you huh?* And that was that. I might as well sit and wait for the search party to come find me and haul me off. Instead of sitting, I wandered around for 20 minutes or so trying to come up with a plan. The map was useless at this point.

That's when I heard a loud bullhorn sound followed by the brightest flashlight I've ever seen being used as a spotlight to cut through the darkness of the woods. *Had I just time-traveled to the next day and this was an actual search party out looking for me?* That's when a voice came over the bullhorn after the fifth siren or so and said, "ANYONE LEFT ON THE COURSE, COME TO THE SOUND OF MY VOICE AND SIT ON THE ROAD. WE WILL COME TO GET YOU." *There's a fucking road nearby?!?!* Sure enough. I turned to my left and followed the light for about 2 minutes until there was a nice dirt road just wide enough for a work truck to fit down. *Damn old lady, you couldn't have just pointed at the dirt road and told me to walk on it while I'm lost at least?*

Nonetheless, I got on the back of the truck along with another half dozen or so lost souls and was driven back to where the tryout started. Back to that empty grass field where we took the PT test. On the way back, all of us lost souls had a good laugh at how dark it was and how hard it was to navigate when you had no earthly idea how to use a map and compass. Glad I wasn't alone. Once we got back and gathered together, I looked around and all I saw was happiness on every face. It was a sense of accomplishment that we all went through something tough together. A sense that even though some of us hadn't seen combat as we had hoped, this was tough and we all made it through on the other side.

It may come as a shock to some of you, but I didn't get chosen to be on the Best of MP team. I know, I know. I guess my unit just didn't see the value I could bring with my expertise in downloading torrents, mopping floors, and driving around in a patrol car writing pointless tickets all day. Bummer for them.

I learned that not being 100% prepared for something is okay sometimes and that everything has a natural tendency to work itself out in the end. I learned that even getting punched in the face by a big Kool-Aid Man isn't so bad when you know other people around you are getting punched in the face, too. Together.

CHAPTER 19: THE B'S

"Why is there smoke coming from under your door?"

—A sergeant to a private right now in a barracks somewhere

The barracks. Where do I even start? The barracks are the perfectly fucked-up mixture of prison, office building, laundry mat, brothel, bar, and tattoo shop. The barracks are their own standalone entity that belongs to the people that live inside of them. Only us non-special forces troops that are a part of the big military get to experience the barracks. Green berets definitely don't stay in them and neither do SEALs, Recon Marines, or PJs. It's a real shame too, because living in the Bs is an experience unlike no other. An experience that leaves a lasting mark on all that come through its doors.

First things first, the barracks are 100% function over form. They're not meant to look pretty, have unique features, or elicit any sort of joy from anyone. Barracks have two purposes and two purposes only: work and sleep. Think of a college dorm, but with your classroom and dean's office downstairs from the room you lived in. Imagine if your apartment was on the fifth floor and the office you went into every day for work was on the ground floor. That's a barracks building.

The barracks that I got the opportunity to live and work in was a three-story, square building straight out of the Eastern Bloc. Unassuming stucco gray exterior, concrete floors inside, and off-white walls all around. If you look up pictures of the interior of a prison you would get the same cold, institutional feel as the barracks I got to stay in. Our rooms were slightly larger than prison cells; each room measuring 10ft by 10ft with a sink and mirror in the corner of your room. Each room shared a toilet and shower with the adjacent room. There were two windows per room and no central air conditioning or heating, rounding out the modern spartan living conditions. You quickly got used to it though because they're all you got. At least it was a free roof over your head with running water and a hot shower (most of the time). Having your military work offices just downstairs made for some frustrating times, to say the least. Having to go up and down the stairs to go stand outside of an office for 30 minutes just to sign your name on a piece of paper. We all know that it didn't mean anything and was the preferred form of torture by anyone with rank over us barracks dirtbags.

Pop quiz: What is the energy source that powers every barracks building in the military today? I'll give you 30 seconds to think of your answer…Ok fine, I'll just tell you. The energy source that powers every barracks building in the military today is a three-pronged energy source: tobacco, alcohol, and body odor. They mix together perfectly to keep the power on in each building and essentially keep the military gears turning.

Alcohol is an obvious fuel source, especially in Germany. The legal drinking age is 18 years old and there's always a cheap liquor store (the Shoppette/gas station) that has any liquor or beer you could ever dream of. You've got a steady paycheck coming in from Uncle Sam so why not go spend 30 bucks on a fifth of Jack. Oh, and throw in that pack of Newports while you're at it. You're rich by your standards back home! Might as well go take that bottle of Jack upstairs to your friend's barracks room and play Call of Duty Modern Warfare. Drink it out of a red solo cup while you are at it, right? Right. Might as well start playing your music loud when you're a couple of drinks in, right? Right. Once the loud music turns on, it's like a bird call to all the other barracks dirtbags that it's party time. Before you know it, you've got a dozen soldiers crammed in a 10x10 space while chain-smoking cigs out of the window. (Smoking is technically prohibited inside the barracks but if you blow the smoke out of an open window it doesn't count. Promise.) That's where the really good ideas start coming into play. *We should wrestle. We should fight. We should go get more booze. We should go out downtown.* All ideas that have been had in a barracks room since the beginning of time.

I had a nice 3-month stint or so where my suitemate, the person in the room adjacent that I shared the toilet and shower with, was the king of all of the above. He was part of our larger company that had just gotten back from Iraq. The Army wouldn't let them patrol the mean streets of Germany with us, cause PTSD and stuff, I guess? They were also moving the entire company to Ft. Bliss in El Paso, TX soon. Both of those things combined meant that fifty or so people that lived in the barracks had fuck all to do but party. Reyes was one of these fifty. Every night, he would go down, get booze, come back up, and play his newly bought thousand-dollar sound system on a level ten. Loud music in the barracks is like moths to a bright light, soldiers can't help themselves. They know there's booze and bad decisions in there, so they fly right into danger like mosquitos flying into that blue light. The typical Call of Duty games and loud heavy metal music would always happen next door, but some nights the music never stopped. Those nights were the real special ones. Luckily the military inadvertently taught me how to sleep wherever and whenever so I was usually able to sleep right through the nightly drunken debauchery. Even with Nickelback and Five Finger Death Punch playing at an eleven just 5 feet away. I knew I was in for a real treat when I woke up and the music was still on next door. That meant that someone or multiple someones had passed out, er, fallen asleep before they were able to crawl over and turn the sound system off. By the way, who actually needs a sound system in a ten-by-ten room? Someone who's a good time, that's who! Moving on.

Once I opened my sleepy little eyes and heard that music through the thin walls that separated my bed from the one next door, the hunt for sprawled-out bodies began. Half sleepwalking to the sink in my room to splash cold water on my face, I could usually already smell the Red Bull, Vodka, and hint of Jägermeister. Always the drink of choice from the parties next door that probably only ended a few hours ago. Other than the music still playing, there was one other key indicator that people—or multiple people—were passed out next door: the shared door into the toilet and shower room was locked from the inside. When you need to use the toilet or shower in the barracks you lock the door leading into your suitemate's room so nobody could get in from that side. With the music still playing and the door locked from the inside, you then have to start figuring out if there's a body on the other side of said door. The first step is getting the door unlocked. This was easy enough with a quarter. You just slide the quarter into the notch and turn with some downward pressure. That releases the deadbolt and you're in.

Now that the door's unlocked, you slowly open it to feel if there's any resistance from the other side. There have been plenty of times where the music has still been on, the door was locked, and there was resistance on the other side. You just have to slowly keep opening until you've pushed the body hard enough. They'll eventually wake up and either walk away or roll over just enough for you to use the bathroom. Maybe, just maybe there was a little throw-up surprise for you in the toilet, but only if you were lucky. It was even possible to find somebody passed out headfirst in the shower with their clothes still soaking wet. It was really the Wild West on the other side of that door once you unlocked it.

I know what you're thinking, and you are right. It is gross to pass out in a shared bathroom with your head on the piss-covered floor, and throw-up in the toilet, but that's life in the barracks baby. You better wake up and drink a Monster Energy because you gotta do it again the next day.

Energy drinks are the perfect remedy for that hangover from the night before. Don't you worry, the Shoppette has plenty of them waiting for you when you get up and at 'em. The barracks, alcohol, and energy drinks: matches made in heaven. You have young, single people with steady paychecks, cheap booze, a new environment, potential anxiety, and trauma from serving in the military, and a steady flow of people that you live with that have the same things.

There was one night in particular that really stands out from the regularly scheduled heavy metal, chain-smoking, pass-out-in-the-bathroom parties next door. That particular day, the party started a little earlier in the night. In fact, the sun was still shining a beautiful golden hue through the windows and the music was only at an eight instead of an eleven. Then there was a knock on my side of the shared bathroom door. *Hmmm, I don't really get invited to the ragers anymore. I wonder what's up?* On the other side was my suite mate, Reyes, with bright eyes and some pep in his eye. He invited me to his room because, "WE'RE GETTIN' INKED UP ALL NIGHT OVER THERE, BRO!" My eyes went wide and started fluttering and I managed to eke out an "ohhhh" and a, "I'll stop by later, but I probably won't get anything."

Boy, oh boy, was I glad that I did stop by later though. It was a scene that I can only imagine is replicated in a prison cell anywhere across the world. The "tattoo artist" was some random dude I'd never seen before that was still wearing his uniform pants, boots, and tan t-shirt. The tattoo gun was a less than stellar mixture of thrown-together parts that included but were not limited to the outer sleeve of a pen, what appeared to be a sewing needle, a copper guitar string, and some sort of small motor with wires hanging off it. A real-life prison setup and I was going to sit there and watch in amazement.

For the next hour, I watched Reyes get a chest piece tattoo that was hard to make out but slightly resembled a skull with smoke coming from its "ears." The tattoo artist and he were sharing a red solo cup filled with Jack Daniels when I slowly walked out of there. The next day, Reyes proudly showed me his finished work of "art" with the words "DEATH BEFORE DISHONOR" added on top of his skull. It looked magnificently horrible–like prison tattoos are supposed to– and ended up lasting about a week before some of the ink started falling out. Perfect for a barracks tattoo.

Time for another pop quiz: What do you get when you mix alcohol with young, single people that are far away from home, living on their own for the first time, in a foreign country, a sense of impending doom over everyone; and males and females all under the same roof? I'll give you a tick.

Tick over. You end up having everyone having sex with everyone, that's what. Guys with girls, guys with guys, girls with girls, guys with girls and guys—a degenerate's dream come true. All in one featureless building spanning across every military base in the world. Everyone in my building belonged to the same little MP unit so not only did we all live together, but we all worked together too. We were unable to escape each other. Naturally, there was drama that went with all the sexcapades going on under that easter bloc looking roof. There was an almost daily report via the Sham Squad on who was having sex with who and who hated who because of who so and so had sex with last night.

Who was seen coming out of whose room late last night or early this morning was constantly the talk at morning chow. Whose wife got too drunk last night and was seen with who at what bar. It was our very own reality show full of twists and turns, backstabbing, betrayal, lust, love, and intrigue. We won't talk about any specific stories(yet), but I would be remiss not to teach you what a barracks rat is. A barracks rat is someone that is always around the barracks and involved in the barracks parties and sexcapades with various people at all times. They could actually live in that particular barracks building, they could be military that live in another barracks building, they could be a family member of a military member, or they could be a local that's not involved in the military except for being a barracks rat. Rats are everywhere, so heads on a swivel, everyone.

Chapter 20: The Fifth Dimension

"Is that a dead body?"

–Every time anyone walks into a barracks laundry room

This next part is the most sensitive in the book and one that the government definitely doesn't want you to know. If you don't want to get caught up in it all, then skip this part and read on, I'll understand.

Okay, you stayed, good.

In every barracks building exists another dimension. Portals that open up into whole other galaxies and worlds complete with the spaceships to take you there. Okay, maybe not all *that* but the laundry room in my barracks building– and those like it–are WILD places. They act as much more than just somewhere to wash and dry clothes. Now that I think about it, the washers and dryers don't even really do that very well so maybe they are actually portals to another dimension. I've never seen them transport someone through time and space like Matthew McConaughey in *Interstellar*, but I don't have 24/7 eyes on the room, so I don't *really* know.

In our building, we were fortunate enough to have two such laundry rooms, both equally wild and crazy. What should we really expect? The laundry room is a place where over a hundred wild-ass soldiers have to share in order to get all of their nasty-ass clothes washed. Our laundry rooms were on the first floor and before you even opened the door and walked in you knew you were in a different dimension. There was a permanent glow coming from around the door anytime you walked by as if Pachamama herself was calling out to passersbys. The brightest summer day with the sun beaming through the hallway outside the laundry room couldn't match the illumination and energy radiating through the gaps in the door.

As soon as you walked into the laundry room, you'd be blinded by the seemingly endless amount of fluorescent lights that are on the ceiling. The entirety of the rest of the building's lighting doesn't add up to these things. They're not the type of lights that have the little diffusing sheet or the weird cage thing that at least pretends to give a shit about our eyes. Did they just have leftover lights when they were building this thing and just figured people needed to see how dirty their clothes were when they were putting them in the washing machine, so they just threw them haphazardly into the laundry rooms? The next thing you'll notice when you're inside is the low hum of dryers seemingly doing their jobs, but wait right there. What is that metal clanking noise that is slightly louder than the typical dryer hum? Glad you asked, that is most definitely the sound of a washer or dryer that's on the verge of exploding and bringing down the first level of the building. Don't worry, the proper maintenance requests have been put in to try and fix said washer or dryer but *shrugs* that's the military way–don't fix shit that's essential for anyone to live a semi-normal life.

Once your eyes adjust to the fourth dimension and you get used to the low hum bomb sound, you can finally take the leap with a full step through the threshold. You're immediately met with a smell that surprises your senses and changes ever so slightly every time you make the journey into the other dimension–known as the laundry room. It's a combination of knock-off Tide detergent, body odor that is embedded in the ceiling tiles, dryer sheets, lint, stale beer, and just a hint of throw-up in the trash can in the corner. How could that smell even be possible? You notice all the windows are open and a breeze is coming through, but that breeze isn't doing shit. It is just making it frigid in there at all times, no matter what the weather is outside. *Okay, so weather patterns don't apply in this dimension*, you think to yourself.

It may take a minute or two, but once your senses are aligned and you've grounded yourself, you start your hunt for an open and operational washing machine to start your journey. And what a journey it is. There are eight total washers and eight total dryers, divided into two rows each so you look down the first row for the chosen one. The telltale sign if a washing machine is open and operational is if there is a pile of clothes (in or out of a laundry basket) directly on top of it…but it's complicated. If the clothes on top of the washing machine are wet, then that means that they were in the washing machine too long and someone just took them out and put them on top instead of actually drying them for the person. It's a dawg-eat-dawg world in the laundry room. If the clothes on top are dry, but seemingly clean, then you're clear to engage and throw your pile in the washing machine.

You must also mind the signs. This means there's a chance that there's a ragtag sign that was printed off Microsoft Paint in 1998 that reads "oUT OF ORDeR" --exactly like that. But again, it's complicated. You must investigate further, young Padawan, for the tape can deceive you. You must look closely at the tape that's holding up the sign. If the tape is halfway melted into the machine, then that machine is in fact out of order. If it's fresh tape—that looks like it isn't quite as sticky as it once was—then it's a fraud. Someone is actually just using that machine as their personal machine. They're going to come use that machine later on and want to ensure it is available. When you find the fraud sign, you have to decide to use that particular machine at your own risk. It could be a bluff and that machine is actually out of order OR maybe someone wants you to think it's *in* order. As I said, it's complicated. You're playing four-dimensional chess.

Once you find a washing machine that actually works and throw your clothes in with a full cap of Tide (no matter the size of the load), you go back up to your room. Now you have to not-so-patiently wait the 45 minutes or so for the wash cycle to finish. Don't wait too long or your clothes will suffer the dreaded wet toss on the floor or on top of the washing machine maneuver. That person just *had* to use that machine right then and there. Dawg-eat-dawg. The same "rules" from the washing machines apply to the dryers: signs, piles of wet or dry, and clean or dirty clothes are stacked on top of every dryer. You finally pick the dryer that is calling out to you from the ether, but careful my young ones, the heating mechanism in that beauty of a machine could be out. If it is out, you could come to get your clothes in 2 hours and realize that they just spun round and round at room temp the whole time. Summed up: there is a less than 50/50 chance of having a washer and dryer open and operational at any particular time. Maybe that's why there are so many nasty-ass uniforms running around the military. What do you expect when the washers and dryers don't work?

The laundry room is so much more than just half-working machines though. There is always someone in there providing some form of entertainment as well. *Always.* The laundry room dimension attracts the best kind of dirtbags the military has to offer. It's a neutral room, a home base of sorts. None of your bosses are going into the laundry room, and why would they? It's just a bunch of smelly-ass clothes and broken machines in there, right? Winky Face. Since we all mostly had roommates in the barracks, the laundry room turned into a quasi-phone booth. It was the only spot in the whole building with some sort of privacy.

The door was thick, the low rumble of the machines was loud enough to cover your voices, and the lights were so bright you could see anybody eavesdropping outside the door. Barracks rats thrived in the laundry room dimension. You could always find one nearby trying to peddle their wares on you. Some of the sexual escapades we talked about earlier definitely happened in the laundry dimension. It did in fact have all the privacy attributes needed to not be the headline story of the Sham Squad the next day. But the Sham Squad always sees, always knows.

You never knew what you would find when you stepped through the door and into the laundry room dimension. It could be empty with every machine available, letting you have a peaceful clothes-washing experience. It could also be filled with a little party serving Jäger and Red Bull, filling your nostrils with the smell of Irish Pub. Of course, all of this was just making the floor more sticky. There could even be a little top-of-the-dryer sex action going on. Sometimes they wouldn't even stopafter you make eye contact while putting your clothes in a washing machine next to them. *Excuse me while I just put my clothes in here real quick.* Wild times. I found someone passed out in the middle of the room more than a few times.

If you're lucky, there could be a full-on fistfight happening right between the washers you are trying to use to wash your nasty ass uniform. *Excuse me gentleman, I'll just squeeze in right here.* A few other instances I have had in this vortex included...

- Someone trying to sneak a girl through the windows past the fire guard.
- A couple screaming at each other as they are breaking up for the seven thousandth time.
- Seeing a pool of blood with no clue how it got there.
- Shit, you might even finding some ammo or an M4 in there, which was absolutely not supposed to be there.

It was a roll of the dice every time you just wanted to wash your drawers. Eventually you get used to it and the laundry room becomes a hot tub time machine. Time didn't exist like it normally does—minutes were hours and seconds were minutes. The laundry room dimension is arguably the most essential part of the world that is the barracks.

CHAPTER 21: HENNESSY TRAIL

"Why does this snow smell like Hennessy?"

—Survivors of the Hennessy Trail

The story of the Hennessy Trail is the original inspiration behind this book. I kept telling it at parties anytime someone asked what the military was like. The first draft of the book got lost, but the Hennessy Trail was the very first thing I put time and effort into recounting and writing. I had to make sure this story could live on.

The Hennessy Trail was born at a time where I had decided to not reenlist in the military. I had told the big green weenie that I did not want to pursue a career in the Army anymore and didn't much enjoy its taste in my mouth any longer. When you do this, you typically won't get sent to any more career-advancing schools—or in other words, not have any more government funds spent on you than is not absolutely necessary. For me, though, that wasn't the case. I think it was so I could one day write about what I was able to experience. Nonetheless, my unit gave me 12 hours of notice that I was going to be going to a school called Warriors Leaders Course, WLC for short.

WLC is a course for young inspiring soldiers that want to get ahead and advance their careers in the military (I was neither). It's a course that teaches you how to be a leader in the Army—from tactics to paperwork—and any non-commissioned officer in the

Army has been to and passed WLC. You're probably wondering why would the Army waste money on teaching someone how to be a leader when they're not going to be around in a few months anyways? Great question. At this point in my military career, I had learned not to even try to make sense of it all and just go with the flow. It would hurt your brain trying to apply logic to a decision like this, so you're better suited to just nod your head and start looking over the packing list.

Oh, don't worry, there was a packing list. Always is. And if we know anything about packing lists, it's that you will never have every item on there. I began the process of wheeling and dealing my way through the barracks in order to get all of the items I needed. I felt like a door-to-door insurance salesman knocking on every door in the barracks asking for a cup of sugar. By the time I got everything all packed up and ready to go I was able to get a few hours of sleep. I still pretty much had zero knowledge of what WLC actually was. All I knew was that I was going to the mountainous part of Germany for 10 days to learn some stuff. Before I knew it, I was in another Sprinter van with a Monster Energy drink, headed to the mountains.

As per usual in the military, you don't just show up to a place and get going with whatever you're there to do. No, no, no, you have to hurry up and wait around for at least half the day. When we first pulled into the base in the middle of the mountains, we asked the very basic question, "Where do we need to sign in for WLC?" Not shockingly, the answer was, "somewhere over there". Off to a great start. I finally found my way to the check-in area– which was the base chapel (church). The chapel was like a refugee camp; some people were sleeping on the floor with just their duffle bags and others were sitting in the pews talking to each other. *Was I in the right spot? The only thing getting checked in here were the insides of eyelids.* So, I did what every good military pro would do, I found a spot on the floor and asked the nearest person what the hell was going on.

"There's only one person checking us all in and they have to go through all of your paperwork to make sure you're actually allowed to be here," was the answer I got from the nearest bro who instantly fell back asleep after giving me the answer. I was too scared to ask how long he had been waiting for his turn, so I settled into what I assumed was going to be a nice little wait. There's an interesting thing with the military and it's that nobody actually knows how time works. Nobody knows how long very basic tasks actually take to complete. Everyone just estimates and ends up leaving grownups waiting around for something to start. Not only are you waiting around doing nothing, but you are being yelled at not to be late. You better be early and you better be ready to go when that time rolls around.

After settling into my little spot on the ground, I picked up that everyone is getting checked in alphabetically by their last name. This means I had plenty of time to take a little nap since we were only on Ls. I woke up and we were much closer, so I pulled out my inch-thick manilla folder of "necessary" paperwork and got ready to actually check in—only 2 hours after I had gotten there. Real efficient. Eventually my name finally got called and I got to experience why a simple check-in process was taking so long. They looked over every single piece of paperwork. My social security number was confirmed on every page, PT test results were verified, a copy of my two forms of photo ID was made. My goodness. Was I checking into the Vatican here or am I just going to learn some basic military leadership things? Either way, I was finally given the go-ahead and hopped on a shuttle bus that took me to our training area.

Once I got to the training area, there was someone in charge that assigned me my cabin and room inside that cabin. I was told to unpack and wait until somebody came to get me for lunch. The training area was like a compound of different buildings for different types of training. There was a DFAC (cafeteria), gym, tiny little Shoppette, and all of our cabins. The cabin area had a total of ten cabins with five in a row on one side, five in a row on the other, and a big open area in the middle of the two rows. Each cabin had five rooms—two people per room—and two bathrooms; do the math and that's 10 people for two bathrooms.

If you think you can just unpack and throw your stuff in the closet, then you are mistaken my friend. You have to unpack according to the diagram pictures that have been placed everywhere inside your room; down to the way your tan underwear is folded and put inside a drawer. That's right, folded tighty-whities—it's a thing, look it up. I met my roommate and he was a nice enough guy, but the real fun started when it was lunchtime. Everyone that was in my WLC class came out of their cabins and gathered up in the big area in between them. It was the dead of winter in the mountains of Germany which means the temperature was in the teens and there was snow on the ground. Weather doesn't matter in the military though. There was a group of a dozen or so guys that didn't give one single shit and were wearing their normal uniforms: no jackets or anything. They were just ripping cigs and laughing, typical hooligans. I was naturally drawn to them, so I made sure I got behind them when it was time to line up for lunch.

Our DFAC for WLC was right there next to our cabins, but the line to get in and actually order was out the door. That's where I learned what a tanker in the Army was. Standing outside in the snow just waiting to get inside to eat a chicken sandwich. It was like the first time you saw your favorite teacher out in public. You always thought they're so cool and now you actually get to see them out in the wild and maybe, just maybe, you would get to talk to them.

For the first 5 minutes I just stood in the line, I didn't say one word. I was just a fly on the wall soaking in the aura of the group. These guys seemed like the inspiration for that Toby Keith song that plays in my head when I'm feeling super high speed. Hell, these guys *are* the Toby Keith song in the flesh. I could tell just by looking at them, they'd definitely put a boot in someone's ass cause it's the American way.

Finally, the main one out of the group–who had seemingly smoked an entire pack of Camel Lights while we were standing there–turned to me and introduced himself before going into a whole rundown of the group. He was an actual corn-fed boy from Nebraska and his group was a mix of tankers and infantrymen that had just gotten back from deployment. The tankers were separated from the infantrymen by their cool boots. Their boots had buckles instead of laces and a hint of jet fuel that seemed to stain their uniforms. Nebraska, as we will call him, says they all got bribed by their unit into coming to WLC right after deployment. He said that if they came, they would get another free week of leave right after. That blew my mind at the moment, that someone would actually drop their whole life just to come to the middle of the mountains and learn some Army leadership stuff. It's like the group could sense my wonderment. The tallest one out of the bunch, who was a Marlboro Red kinda guy, chimed in and assured me that they were here to get fucked up too. I didn't know that was going to be such a premonition but boy, oh boy, would that tall skinny guy turn out to be a real Machiavelli. These guys in this group felt like the real salt of the earth, no BS type of soldiers that I was hoping for when I joined the Army.

The next morning at breakfast, much to my excitement, I got invited to sit at the cool kids' table with the tankers and infantry guys. This is where the real stories started to pour out and I was just sitting there taking it all in. Honestly, star-struck a little bit. One of them pulled out their Blackberry (RIP Blackberries) and showed me a video of one of their tanks running over a concrete barrier somewhere in Iraq then firing the big gun and leveling a building. Of all the messed-up videos I had seen on the internet, tank battles had not been among them, so I was shocked at the pure power and ferocity of a modern tank. Before the end of breakfast, I learned that the tall skinny Marlboro Red guy had actually "smoked," a.k.a. killed a top ten terrorist in Afghanistan with a 240B machine gun. The nonchalant way they told that story really opened my eyes to the realities of war. It showed me that I was interacting with soldiers who had been hardened by combat. They talked about death and war at the breakfast table as casually as you talk to your wife about the weather that day. The only killing I ever did in the military was killing a 36 oz Monster energy and mopping an entire floor of the barracks. So, we're all basically the same, right?

The whole rest of the week there was an energy coming from the tanker group that screamed *we're going to party and party hard this weekend.* Well, less of an energy and more of a statement they made every chance they got. Making an ambush plan on a sand table? *Can't wait to get fucked up this weekend.* Learning to call in a 9-line Medevac out in the middle of the woods? *Can't wait to blackout this weekend.* Standing in line to get another chicken sandwich at dinner? *Two more days until the weekend.* They were ready to go when Friday afternoon finally rolled around. We got briefed on the rules of the weekend: can't leave the base, be back inside our little training compound by 1900 (7 p.m., come on, you still don't know?), don't go anywhere alone, don't get into any trouble while you're out doing stuff. Then the gold rush happened.

Before I even knew what was going on, all the tanker crew were power walking out of our compound headed to the Shoppette, backpacks on every one of their backs. *Hmmm, why backpacks?* Well, silly. So, they can carry as much booze and tobacco as humanly possible. There was an entire bar of options when we got back. This was a whole other level of booze than even I was used to, and that's saying a lot. My roommate got run over when he was drunk and had to go to rehab. I had to physically move my barracks neighbor with a door after he passed out on the bathroom floor. My resume is thick. But this? This seemed different. This seemed like a gravitational pull that I wouldn't be able to resist, no matter my effort. That evening I went into my cabin and made sure my underwear was still folded properly (it was, thank goodness) and closed my little eyes. I got a solid ten hours of sleep, like the golden boy that I was. The next morning, I was anticipating people to be passed out all over the place with throw-up in the snow–stuff from the Hangover movie.

I went outside to get some fresh morning air and try to find some cell phone reception. I was expecting to be the first one up and moving around, but much to my surprise, the tanker crew was already standing outside casually smoking and drinking coffee. They were acting like it was a slow Saturday morning in New York City. *How is this possible?* They had backpacks full of fifths in every liquor imaginable. I thought that one of the group members might actually be dead by morning, so I was visibly shocked to see them up and functioning like normal humans.

"Just a warmup," one called as I walked by. I wanted to stop and get details, but I needed to keep looking for a couple of bars of cell service. I needed to call bae back in the States and see if we were married yet or not. Oh yeah, forgot to mention, my wife and I got married while she was back in the States and I was in Germany. In Texas, you can have an absentee marriage ceremony. This just means that you don't physically have to be together to have a marriage ceremony and become legally married. It's meant for prisoners, but bae and I used it so we could get married and start our life together. She was submitting our paperwork and signing the marriage certificate that day. I wanted to stay in touch, so I knew if I was officially a married man or not. Seemed important. I digress.

After I finally found a spot that threw me a bar of service, I found out bae was still asleep. Not married. I started slogging back through the snow to the cabin area to grab some coffee of my own. We were all under the impression that WLC was a gentleman's course; meaning that nobody was going to yell at you. Cadres (people in charge) were there to teach us, not to babysit us, right? We were going to get treated like grown-ups, right? Weekends were supposed to be free time to do whatever you want as long as nobody got arrested or died. That Friday afternoon the cadre reaffirmed that and just told us to have a morning accountability formation. That way they could make sure that everyone was present and accounted for from the night before. Seems easy enough to me. I grabbed my coffee and went to stand in formation—we had everyone and that was that.

Most of us ate our breakfast at the DFAC and then went to hang out around the cabin area. It was starting to snow pretty hard outside, so there was nothing else really to do. That snow day is really where my Sham Squad membership really shined. I whipped out my laptop and had the latest movie theater releases ready to stream so fast that nobody even knew what was happening. Hiding my VPN and finding the pirating sites with the best quality was a specialty of mine back "home". I was proud to show off my skills in front of all my new friends. I don't even know what movies we watched that day but it was definitely a sight to see—like out of a Hallmark movie. Ten or so soldiers huddled around a little laptop watching a shaky video camera quality movie without a care in the world. A little after lunch, everybody went back to their own rooms for afternoon nap time. But as the main tanker guy walked out, he tapped me on the shoulder and said, "You know we were just getting warmed up last night, right? We hadn't drank since before deployment, so we didn't want to get too shit-faced. Tonight, we rage," and then he just walked off. Was that an invitation or was that just a public service announcement? I stood there frozen and just nodded my head as he walked away and lit a cig before he even got out of the cabin. Damn, these guys are cool.

Chicken sandwich dinner comes and goes again, and I do my thing after. I go to the gym, shower up, read a little Brad Thor, before starting to get ready for bed. As I was laying down my little head and about to close my eyes on that fateful Saturday night, God intervened. Bae texted me and asked me to call her. That's how our long-distance phone system worked back then. She would text me to call her and then I would find a landline to call her back on. The military land lines that usually had free calling to the United States, but they were in the barracks. It helped save us money on the long-distance calling charges and allowed us to actually talk and build a relationship together. Anyways, she texted me to call her, so I was up out of bed and back outside. I was on the hunt for some bars to be able to call her from my cell phone this time since there were no landlines. Don't worry, I made sure to load up my Blackberry with enough minutes so I could still use it while I was in the middle of the mountains.

After finding a bar or two out in the middle of the snow, I got to confirm with bae that indeed I was not officially married yet. I turned off my phone and headed back down to my warm cabin for night-nighttime. My time on the snow hill cup caking with bae had been about an hour or so. By the time I got back down to the cabins, it was a whole new world. The cabin that all the tankers and infantrymen were staying in was directly across the open area from mine and it was THUMPIN. There was loud music coming from it and all the lights were out. You could see lighters sparking up, and there was smoke coming out of the cracked windows. I stood outside of their last cabin in disbelief. These guys really are straight out of a Captain America cartoon. After a couple of minutes spent in awe and admiration, I shook off the snow from my beanie and started trudging towards my cabin to actually fall asleep and rest up for the next day.

As I was putting my hand on the outside door of my cabin to step inside, I heard a yell from across the open area. It was coming from one of the open smoke-filled windows of the tanker cabin.

"HEYYYOOO, YOU PLAY SPADES?" *Spades? Wtf is Spades? No, I don't play Spades, isn't that for old ladies or some shit? Definitely don't say that though. So, what should we do? What should we do? Think, think, think. Be cool.*

"I don't know how, but I'll fuck with it," was my cool-guy answer., It was met with what seemed like a 5-minute pause, then a "ALRIGHT, GET IN HERE!"

I'M GETTIN CALLED UP TO THE BIG LEAGUES BOYS! This was all I could think about on that 10-second walk across the open space to their cabin. When I got to the door and opened it, I froze and just stood there in utter amazement at what I saw. It looked like a scene out of *The Godfather* and *Friday* combined. Smoke rolled out of the door as if there was a fog machine making it all. A bright light— like the one at the end of the tunnel before you cross over into the afterlife– blinded me as I took in the sweet, sweet aroma of Black and Milds. "CLOSE THE DOOR!" It shook me back into reality and I stepped inside.

I don't remember much but I do remember that I tried Hennessy for the first time. Actually, I helped my new friends finish a fifth of it as well as a pack of Black and Milds. I was fully immersed in the tanker/infantry life and they taught me what a blind nil was as I sang along to Swisher House, Paul Wall, Lil Wayne, and all the other southern rappers you can think of. *This is America. What a time to be alive.* The party went on until almost sunrise. At some point I must have stumbled my way to my room to pass out. I know this because I was rudely awakened by a not-so-pleasant surprise at 0600. It took me five times of saying "huh" to understand why I was being woken up on a Sunday at such an hour. The sixth time is a charm, I guess, and the poor soul who was trying to get me to understand very slowly said, "P.T. Formation. In. Ten". The Henny was still running through me, so I yelled, "FUCK YOU, NO WAY" and tried to go back to sleep. Well, it was true. Everyone was milling about getting ready and I just could not believe the betrayal that was being brought on us like this. We were supposed to have the weekend off. Hence me drinking fucking Hennessy, smoking Black and Milds, and playing spades until God knows how early this morning. This is number one bullshit.

But there we all were, standing outside on the verge of throwing up in the snow just waiting to hopefully do some push-ups and sit-ups and get on out of there. I glanced over to the tankers and infantry guys. They all had shit-eating grins on their faces. It's like they were meant to do PT in the cold, still drunk and tasting like burnt Black and Milds. After 10 minutes of standing around shivering, the final nail in this misery was driven into my back. The expected push-ups, sit-ups, and going back inside to recover from this vicious Henny induced hangover was all a pipe dream. I couldn't believe my drunk ears when the overly enthusiastic cadre said we were going on a team-building log run through the woods. In layman's terms, we were going to run through the woods carrying these huge logs, ammo cans, and water jugs. All in the name of "team building." On a Sunday. In this condition.

We were broken into groups of ten or so and given a 10-foot log, five ammo cans, five 5-gallon jugs full of water, and a 5-mile route through the mountainous forest. All of your team members, logs, cans, and jugs had to cross the line together…go, team! I was quickly put in the tanker team and off we went through the forest, logs and cans in tow. There was fresh powder on the ground and the bright sun was coming up, causing us who finished that bottle of Hennessy to be blinded by the glare. I was in the first group to carry the log. Having that log on my shoulder felt like I was carrying an elephant. I should still be sleeping off this massive hangover right now, but instead, I feel like my body is made of paper and is going to crush under the weight of this damned log at any time.

Now, I already had a headache before even picking up the log and attempting to run with it. But now, that seemingly thousand-pound log had turned it into an *"Omg. Did that log penetrate my skull and just crush my brain?" type of headache. Am I dead?* Don't worry, we didn't just throw that thing up on our shoulders like it was nothing. No, no, no. It actually took us a couple of times because we were too drunk and hungover to have the strength and coordination to do it quickly. Once we got it, we were off. Not in a straight line, of course, but along a winding little snake path in the snowy dirt road. It didn't take long before we had to drop the log and let the first person puke up some remnants of the night before. At least it was a form of entertainment to me and of the rest of the group. *Half a mile in and already taking a puke break. This might take a while, coach.* No, we are SOLDIERS. Time to HOOOOOAH up and get it done.

For the next hour or so we swapped out roles—who was carrying the log, who was dragging the water jugs, and who was dry heaving. If it was your turn to dry heave, you got a couple of good ones in and then ran back up to the group to catch up. Once we all got a good sweat going, the smell on the trail turned from fresh mountainous pine candles to Hennessy with a touch of Black and Milds. Smelling the Hennesy sweat from our bodies, made us puke even more—it was a real circle of life moment there for the last 3 miles or so. But at least we were doing it together. Running off the vicious hangover right next to each other.

Our lungs were burning, both from the dry heaving and how hard this actually was. But to me, it felt like we were the real Band of Brothers—out here in the German mountains, working together to stay alive. Yeah, stay alive. My tanker brothers were out here struggling and I needed to make sure they got home safe from this. Okay, maybe I was being a *little* dramatic. There probably weren't any Nazis hiding in the forest waiting to kill us all. This also wasn't the first or last time these tankers were doing some horrendous PT hungover. At least we were managing to laugh about it.

At the end of our 5-mile run, our arms were aching, our lungs were burning, our mouths were dry as ever, and our clothes were soaked in sweat. Sweat that smelled like we washed our clothes in liquor, but I digress again. After we were able to breathe and stand up, we dubbed that 5-mile loop the "Henny Trail.". We then promptly went to the DFAC and devoured all the hangover food you could imagine– biscuits and gravy, omelets, pancakes, orange juice, and half a gallon of coffee each. We then passed out until about noon with smiles on our faces.

We all graduated WLC the following weekend. We then had to leave each other to go back to our separate bases and separate lives. I stayed in touch with a few of the tanker crew, but time did what it always does in the military. Who knows what those crazies are doing today. Oh! I do know that one of the Henny Trail veterans–the one who had MOB with a big dollar sign tattooed on his hand–became a rapper in Louisiana. I rocked with his stuff for a second there. Other than that, nothing. Just know that if you come across someone who is or was a tanker–they're crazy.

CHAPTER 22: HURRY UP AND WAIT

"You better be there 15 minutes before the 15 minutes or I'm going to be SO MAD."

–A team leader to their troops

"Hurry up and wait" is defined as a situation in which one is forced to hurry up to complete a certain task or arrive at a certain destination, by a specified time; only for nothing to happen at that time. This definition perfectly wraps up what the non-special forces military looks like. At one point it was even the title of this very book. It's THAT big of a part of the military. Instead of silver stars, purple hearts, and TV deals, we become royalty at standing around. Princesses and princes. Kings and queens. Queen Elizabeth was able to stand in the same spot for 8 hours at a time. She did it by going inward to entertain herself, thinking about God knows what. See, we're the same as the Queen. Royalty that was able to withstand the change of command ceremonies and daily formations. We were experts at standing in the cold (or heat) watching a Colonel or butter bar Lieutenant be late because they were playing touch butt with their friends while us plebs stand around and watch. There should be an entire ribbon stack for all the pointless formations that we had to endure. Paragraphs of our resumes should read something like, "Is able to endure countless meetings that should have been an email". That's exactly what formations are. This could have been a text, come on!

The formation is the most common way in which anyone in the military will have to "hurry up and wait". Formation is military talk for a meeting. Not the type of meeting that the rest of the "normal" world is accustomed to. This type of meeting is more of the *stand around and get told mostly useless information with no opportunity to speak* type of meeting. Such useless information can include but is not limited to…

- If you're allowed to be done with work for the day.
- You shouldn't drink and drive, get arrested, or light stuff on fire.
- Make sure not to marry any strippers.
- You shouldn't harm your spouse, yourself, your kids, or anybody else.
- Definitely don't get an inappropriate tattoo.
- For sure don't beat each other up.
- Oh, and don't do drugs.

In the military, however, your "meeting," a.k.a. formation, doesn't start on time—ever. Imagine you're sitting in a packed conference room at your job and the entire company is there for a meeting to start. The meeting was supposed to start at 3:30, but now 3:40 comes and goes. Everyone is just chatting with each other and making small talk, but slowly you start to notice some of your coworkers are starting to get restless. Your boss is nowhere in sight and it's now 3:45. The small talk has begun to shift to how ridiculous it is that a professional meeting is starting 15 minutes late. Don't they have any respect for our time? You start thinking to yourself, *I could be doing a dozen other better things than sitting in this conference room waiting for this meeting to start.* "I am about to just leave, what can they do to me!?" is tossed out as a feeler idea by someone to see if anyone would hop try to get more people on board.

At 3:49, the boss finally shows up and everyone that was talking all that shit has to pretend that everything is fine. They have to pretend that they're so happy to be there and can't wait to hear whatever is about to come out of the boss's mouth. That is exactly what happens at every military formation that has ever been since the beginning of militaries. The great Roman armies of centuries ago probably had soldiers standing around doing nothing while they waited on their leaders to come tell them some dumb shit.

Let's break down how every formation goes from start to finish, shall we? First, the hurry-up-and-wait fix is in it from the beginning. In the military there's a saying that goes "On time is late,", meaning you're expected to be there 15 minutes early. FIFTEEN! That's a guaranteed quarter of an hour of your life that is going to be wasted; at the very least. Once a formation time is given by your boss, it's likely that your direct supervisor is going to tell you that you actually have to be there 20 minutes early. "YOu NeVeR kNoW wHaT's GoInG tO hAPpEn!" Okay, fine, 20 minutes of your life wasted now. Gone forever.

Second, you're going to show up to formation 20 minutes early and everyone is going to start gathering into cliques or groups. Even if you're not a smoker or dipper, you're going to be standing around a group that is so might as well get used to it. While we wait, everyone is generally just talking shit about how shitty the military is. Connecting on how we can't wait till we get out of this hellhole, you know, normal healthy conversations. Standing around in groups during these first 20 minutes or so until the formation is actually supposed to start is when people start roasting each other. Name-calling, your momma jokes, how they never should have been in the military in the first place. Classic friends' stuff, ya know?

Third, about 5 minutes before the formation is supposed to start, a sergeant will look at their watch and say, "Well, guess we better line up." And everyone will look at their own watches or phones and say, "Yep, guess so." Every time, without fail. It still happens to this day, I bet. Then everyone puts out their cigs and begrudgingly starts the slow walk over to where the formation is to happen. Before you know it, we're all standing in loose rows of about ten or so. Our shoulders slumped in a sort of submissive acceptance of all the time being wasted.

Fourth, it's right at the time this shindig is supposed to start, nothing will ever have actually begun. At go time, you'll have a bunch of soldiers just standing around in those loose rows starting to look at our watches and phones every 5 seconds. No matter how many times all of us have been in formation, for some reason *this* time we think it's going to be different. *This* time we think we hurried up for a good reason. *This* time we got here on time, early actually, because the formation was going to start on time. Weaklings.

The start time comes and goes with no sight of our bosses. That's when the mutiny talks really start coming on strong. It's 5 minutes past now and someone around you says they're just going to blow this popsicle stand and there's nothing nobody can do about it.

"This is ridiculous."

"Waste of our time."

"I've got better things to be doing than standing around waiting on these chop dicks."

"I'm about to just pack my shit and leave for good."

All things that are said at every. single. formation. But nobody is going to go anywhere and everyone knows it. It sure is fun to pretend sometimes though, huh?

During this mutiny phase, the fiddling with the uniform part starts to happen. Straightening of name tape, redoing some Velcro, retying your boots. After all, you don't want to look like a schlub while you're standing around doing nothing. This is the phase where the leaders really have to try their hardest not to become bootlickers and join the mob. We all know that they know that we're standing around wasting time here, but they must remain professional and not fall into the trap of complaining.

The fifth part of a formation is the sighting. The sighting is the part that excites the mob the most. The part that brings the most amount of hope every time. Hope that maybe we'll get to go home early today. Hope that we won't even have to come to work tomorrow. Hope that the person in charge of this formation has somehow turned into the messiah and is coming to unleash us all from the binding contracts we all signed our lives away to and give us each a pot of gold on the way out. That flash of hope happens in a split second when that lieutenant–that's been late to every formation they've been in charge of so far–peaks their head around the corner. For that split second, everyone wants to forgive them of their sins and let them save us. It never happens though. They're all false prophets that will sometimes (maybe) let you off work early, but never baptize you in true waters of freedom.

The sixth part is when you actually get the information. The leader of the formation has finally decided to grace everyone with their presence. They go up in front of everyone and call everyone to attention (a position in the military meaning you stand straight with heels together, hands by your sides in a fist, standing tall, looking straight ahead and staying silent). They might tell everyone to relax, might. Eventually they will start talking. They are mostly start talking just to hear themselves talk most of the time. *You know we all can read, right? Well, you right, MOST of us.* You could have just sent this information via text or email. Hell, maybe even a courier pigeon. I don't need to be standing here for 30 minutes waiting just for *you* to tell me that we need to keep the barracks cleaner or to pick up trash around the building. I just don't, okay? At least get on with it when you're up there and go through your little spiel quickly so we can get out of here.

Part seven is the great exodus. Once the information from part six has been given and the formation is dismissed, it's like the kitchen light being turned on and all the cockroaches start scattering in every direction. People are putting their heads down and walking quickly to ensure they can't get called back for some ungodly reason. If it's an end-of-the-day formation and there's no more work for the day, then there might be a slight jog back to your barracks room to start the night. If it's a Friday and the weekend is upon us, then it's definitely a race back to see who can get the first drink of the nectar of the Gods. Wherever you are going, you're trying to get as far away as possible from the site where you just hurried up and waited. The place where you showed up early, knowing that this stand-around meeting wasn't even going to start on time, much less early, but you did it anyway. The site that you got there early and complained about it the whole time and acted shocked when it started late despite it starting late every time for the past year or so. But that's the game when you hurry up and wait and you have a good time playing it.

We know about formation "hurry up and wait", but we need to talk about the grandest form of hurry up and wait there is in the military: The change of command ceremony "hurry up and wait". The change of command ceremony is just like the regular 'ole formation, but all the seven parts we talked about are turned up to an eleven on the ridiculous scale. First, the change of command ceremony is a big deal in the military and it's where the term "dog and pony show" first got its origins. Okay, maybe not, but it's the perfect definition of a dog and pony show. Change of command is exactly that. Somewhere along the chain of command that you're in, one of your big bosses is leaving and someone is taking their place. When this happens, every soldier that's a part of that person's entire chain of command shows up and stands around in formation. We all have to be there just to see someone we never met hand the keys to the castle over.

You've probably guessed by now, but every single one of those soldiers that are there doesn't give one single shit. They want to be anywhere other than where they're standing right now. A change of command ceremony would be like if your area manager at Walmart—who's in charge of 20 or 30 stores—was going to another area so they mandated that every employee from those 20 or so stores come stand in groups in the parking lot and watch them give a little speech and introduce the new area manager.

The change of command ceremony might actually be where you'll hurry up and wait the most. Instead of having to show up 20 minutes early, how does 45 minutes early sound, chief? And you know it, the complaints are ramped up and spicier than ever during the smoking phase. Instead of shuffling our feet and walking over right before the formation is supposed to start, you have to start standing in actual formation about 20 minutes before it's set to begin. And not in a loose, moving around, or joking around type of way either. No, no, no. You're going to be standing in a very straight line, looking straight ahead with the help of your line leader (a.k.a. squad leader, a.k.a. kindergarten teacher) that has to show you what a straight line is. Now, instead of you messing around with your uniform, fixing little things, your kindergarten teacher is going to do it for you. For this ceremony, you have to wear your change of command uniform, meaning the "nice" uniform out of your bunch of worn-out uniforms. The not-so-dirty one that maybe you've actually washed within the last week.

The time comes and goes for the change of command ceremony, but this time it's different because you have to stand there in a straight line looking straight ahead. It's torture because you can typically see everything that's going on while you're standing out in a big open space like what's used for a change of command ceremony. You see the old boss walking around shaking hands and yucking it up with their friends. You see the new boss just sitting there next to their family. No one is even paying attention to us peasants who are standing there waiting on them. Then the first person falls out. Literally falls out. Falls flat on their face, passed out.

Change of command ceremonies' hurry up and wait is such a larger waste of time because you have to practice standing around and waiting. The day before, everyone gathers and does a "test run" to make sure everyone knows where they have to stand, what they have to do, when to salute, when you should smoke so nobody important sees you, and when not to fart (seriously). You are reminded of the only tip you need to remember so you don't fall over from exhaustion...don't lock your knees. Someone always ends up locking their knees and gives us all some entertainment while we're being bored to death by one of our high-up bosses. They are rambling on about "What an honor it's been to serve this prestigious unit, blah, blah, blah."

The knee-lockers can come from anywhere in the formation and they fall like a great Redwood in the forest. Stiff as a board, not as light as a feather. They come silently crashing down and landing between people. Then the angry whispers come from a sergeant "Get 'em out of here," cause you wouldn't want the bosses to even see one of us peasants struggling. Helping the falling redwood get out of there is also your ticket out of that hell hole, so it's a silent fight to be the one to help them up and out of the formation. Once your new area manager boss makes their little speech, some cannons go off, doves are released into the air (okay, not really but it wouldn't surprise me), and you stay standing there until all the bosses get in their cars and drive off. You've now been standing stiff as a board for more than an hour, dehydrated, and really mad that you had to hear all of this. But you made it, congratulations.

The change of command ceremony "hurry up and wait" should have its own medal in the not-special forces stack. I propose for every five ceremonies you get your time wasted; you get a medal that is all black—the color those ceremonies make your soul.

END OF THE ROAD

"It's not goodbye, it's see ya later."

–Me to you right now

In the big military, you typically move to a different unit and different location every 2 to 3 years. You have 2 years to make memories with a particular group of friends before one or more of you have to leave and likely never see each other again. Everyone says that you'll come together again someday but time keeps on ticking, ticking, into the future. You end up making different friends when you get to where you're going. Out of the dozens of close friends I made in the Army, I may still talk to a couple of them today.

But you and I are different. We've been together from MEPS to basic training all the way to Germany. You've met some ridiculous people, learned what a Sham Squad is, and hopefully laughed with each other along the way. There weren't any Medal of Honor -winning stories of bravery or life-saving feats, but there were plenty of stories about comradery and taking care of each other, (whether you like each other or not). That shared suffering is all you got once you're in the cog that is the big military. And the big military is big. There are over a million people serving, in the military and 99% of them are NOT special forces. Over a million people that Americans swear they "support" but don't even know their everyday stories...until now. If you've been a part of the big military, the not-special forces part of it, I hope you feel heard. I hope you're proud. Now hurry your ass up and wait for the next book to come out. You're crazy if you think those are all the stories I have. Oh, I'm gonna need you there 30 minutes early to wait, though.

Made in the USA
Monee, IL
10 November 2023

46078480R00144